Andrea Paq  nate
journey into ding
of childhood ner own
personal expe. and those of her clients, Andrea
accurately portrays the inner emotional life and challenges
(and) faced by those who have experienced childhood
emotional neglect. Most importantly, she adeptly *names*
these experiences, as they are often "invisible," and exist
as an *absence* of something, rather than as a remembered
traumatic event.

Additionally, *Lovable* has an extensive Healing section,
providing a well-researched, evidence-based roadmap of
tools and practices to support self-healing, self-compassion
and self-expression. These include mindfulness, heart-brain
coherence exercises, visualization, breathwork, body scans
and journaling.

The Healing section is very engaging, practical and
easy to follow. One of the exercises that I found profoundly
helpful, was the "Grounding Visualization." As a nurse I find
that most of my energy is going out to others all day, so I
appreciated the guided experience of *"pulling all of your energy
in from the environment around you—the people, situations and
circumstances,"* so that it was now available to me. It sounds
very simple but was quite seismic in its healing effect.

Lovable is truly a remarkable resource and guide for
helping us "relearn how to live and love with our whole
heart as our authentic selves." This timely book contributes
powerfully to the process of healing and self-transformation
of those with sensitive hearts, and I am thankful to the
Author for bringing this important work to the world.
—*Kathleen M Miller, PhD, RN, AHN-BC, Assistant
Professor at MGH Institute for Health Professions*

The messages in this book are powerful. You show the
negative or hard aspects of each topic and then give ideas,
examples of how to heal and work towards positive behaviors
and self-care. I think this allows the reader to develop a new

idea or skill to learn and share with others with similar symptoms.

My favorite area of the book was the Daily Mindfulness Practice list. This is so needed right now and also such a simple outline to use and follow!

—*Holly Wright, PhD, FNP-BC, Family Nurse Practitioner*

A book containing various real-life examples of how most are affected by the different kinds of neglect parents pass on to their children, leaving wounds to be carried on unknowingly into their adult life. Andrea deconstructs these patterns through the examples and shares holistic practices that can help one to start navigating the journey towards more authentic living with one true self. The collective journey we are currently witnessing.

—*Rebecca Gauci, Artist*

As a healthcare provider, I can tell you that I don't know many women in my practice who don't need to read this book. Andrea is a shining example of somebody who has insight personally and professionally into childhood trauma and the ability to heal. I read the book in a matter of hours because I couldn't put it down. Now I am able to go back to it and utilize the helpful techniques.

—*Vicki Kirby, MSN, FNP-BC, Family Nurse Practitioner*

In a world packed to the rafters with gurus and influencers telling you who you should be, what you should do and how you should do it, this is a cut to the chase revelation of where many of our dissatisfactions stem from in life. Refreshing, powerful and beautifully written, *Lovable* gives you the tools to discover who you are and from that place, the confidence to finally be yourself. It is written for women, however the message of *Lovable* is relevant to us all. A down to earth and practical book with case studies galore, tenderly shared in the safe hands of author Andrea Paquette—it's impossible not to relate if you're on that personal journey of self-discovery. I doubt anyone who is struggling to find purpose and sense of self could put this down without feeling a deep resonance with what is inside the pages. At last, a shining light on the root to emotional struggles rather than just another sticking plaster that says 'fake it 'til you make it'. This is the kind of book that has the power to change lives, permanently. You will want to share it with others, so perhaps it's best to buy a few.

—*Pipa Gordon, Writer and Broadcaster*

What's not to love when a book starts with "I met Amy Gray at the bar...," and that was just in the acknowledgements! I loved reading *Lovable*. Andrea Paquette, the author, offers a soft gentle style to readers in her personal stories and experiences as a holistic nurse that touch the reader's silent, dark, hard places. For those experiencing early trauma, her words are, as Dr. Phil would say, "a soft place to land." *Lovable* answers many questions for women seeking to understand growing up in a complicated and complex family and may question her inner most thoughts, feelings, misunderstandings as a result. The Healing sections after each chapter in the book guide the reader in her search to find true self. You too can be lovable, like Andrea!

—*Julie Pelletier-Rutkowski, MS, RN, Feng Shui practitioner, WSMN radio host of Wicked Healthy Radio.*

I found this book *Lovable* so relatable. I not only saw myself on the pages of this book but also some of my clients, some of my friends and some of the young adults that I have the honor of knowing.

I especially loved the grounding visualization that you did in the chapter about the Overly Sensitive Child. So powerful. The way this book was written will allow you to relate to one if not many scenarios and unlike many other books gives you a powerful process to help you overcome whatever challenges you may have because of it.

—*Deborah Knight, life coach*

Wow. As soon as I read the opening words of *Lovable*, I knew this book was for me. Author Andrea Paquette understands what it's like to be a woman with a sensitive heart. She is incredibly well equipped both personally and professionally to understand and explain the impact of childhood neglect on emotional health and the human soul.

Andrea's account of her own childhood is brave and honest, and her advice for others who have experienced emotional neglect is practical and insightful. Perceptive, compassionate, and deeply empathetic, *Lovable* offers so much to people who have experienced childhood emotional neglect.

When Andrea wrote, "this book will break your heart and then help you mend it," she wasn't kidding. I had tears in my eyes before I even got through the Introduction. I saw myself. But I also felt hope, because I immediately sensed that this book would do more than just make me feel seen; it would also help me heal.

I recommend this book to anyone who wants to bring about self-healing from the wounds of childhood emotional neglect and go forward with strength and hope.
—*Alice Kelly, writer*

LOVABLE

LOVABLE

How Women Can Heal
Their Sensitive Hearts

and Live and Love
as Their True Selves

Andrea Paquette, MSN, APRN
Holistic Nurse Practitioner

Peter E. Randall Publisher
Portsmouth, New Hampshire
2022

Softcover ISBN: 978-1-942155-42-3
Ebook ISBN: 978-1-942155-43-0

Library of Congress Control Number: 2021924235

Peter E. Randall Publisher
Portsmouth NH 03801
www.perpublisher.com

Book design: Grace Peirce

Printed in the United States of America

Credits:

Deepak Chopra, "The Divine Feminine and the Power to Change the World," from *SFGate*, January 27, 2020. Reprinted by permission of Hearst Communications, Inc.

Thomas Hübl, *Healing Collective Trauma* © 2020 Thomas Hübl, excerpted with permission from the publisher, Sounds True, Inc.

Jalal Al-Din Rumi, "The Guest House," from *The Essential Rumi: New Expanded Edition*, translated by Coleman Barks, HarperCollins, 2010. Reprinted by permission of Maypop Books.

Karen Salmansohn (@notsalmon), "Often it's the deepest pain which empowers you to grow into your highest self," Twitter, August 18, 2017, 2:50 p.m., https://twitter.com/notsalmon/status/89861805750507929. Reprinted by permission of the author.

Terri St. Cloud, "the whole" (Bone Sigh Arts, 2003), https://www.bonesigharts.com/store/the-whole. Reprinted by permission of Bone Sigh Arts.

Marianne Williamson, *A Return to Love: Reflections on the Principles of "A Course in Miracles."* Copyright © 1992 by Marianne Williamson. Used by permission of HarperCollins Publishers.

Contents

PART 1
Wounding Experience of Emotional Neglect
in Childhood

PART 2
Coping: Effects of Childhood Wounding in Adulthood

PART 3
Healing: Holistic Healing Plan for Emotional Wounds

~

Acknowledgments

This book has been waiting to be born for many years. I knew I was going to write a book but could never settle on the exact topic. After researching and trying many natural and holistic treatments for my own anxiety and depression, I came across the concept of childhood emotional neglect. It illuminated and clarified my childhood experience so clearly that I knew this would be the perspective from which I would write my book. The following research and writing process became a personal healing journey for me. Along the way I found professionals in the book writing, publishing, and speaking arenas who propelled me on. Even just a sentence or two stating their belief in me and my idea was pivotal in keeping me excited and engaged in the process.

I met Amy Gray at the bar at my favorite local restaurant. Her family sat down beside me and we chatted a bit. I told her what I did for work and how I wanted to bring my ideas to bigger audiences through speaking and writing. Then she told me that she is a speaker agent and she thinks I have something important to offer. Her endorsement of my ideas started me on my path to make my dreams come true. I deeply appreciated Amy's warmth and kindness. I am so grateful for that serendipitous meeting.

Amy recommended I check out Beth Kempton's Book Proposal Master Class. I'm grateful for Beth's supportive and kind demeanor throughout the experience. Along with her rigorous program, I received everything I needed to bring my concept to life. Beth was truly inspiring and as great a role model as she is a successful author herself.

Then when I was ready to partner with an editor, I found Matthew Gilbert on book-editing.com. I truly appreciated his knowledge, expertise, patience, and kindness during my writing process. I had written several compelling stories from my clients' and my own experiences, but I was stuck on how to construct a useful self-help book with this material. I really needed someone to help me organize my ideas and format the book. At first, I was looking for a female editor, thinking she would relate to the book better than a male, but I couldn't pass up Matthew's qualifications. He had so many great suggestions that I would never have thought of as a first-time writer. His perspective challenged and clarified my thought process, wording, and concepts. With his suggestions the book became so much more than I imagined.

While I was writing the book, I submitted my proposal to several publishers. No one was biting. I had consulted Deidre Randall, of Peter E. Randall Publisher, early on, when it was going to be a memoir. She was so encouraging and appreciative of the message I was trying to convey that I started to believe this was a worthwhile project. She was the first person in the book writing and publishing business who told me I had an interesting idea and I was a good writer. I'm so grateful for that initial encouragement. It gave me confidence to keep going. After I finished writing the book and researching many publishing options, I came back to Deidre to publish this book. I couldn't think of anyone I trusted more to bring my book baby into the world.

My sister Pamela Sweeney was living with me during the time I wrote the book. In many little ways, she kept me going, sort of like a mother, asking, "Did you write today?" She always jumped in with any problem I was having, calling on her own experiences and resources to help me out. She contacted an old friend of hers who lead me to the website where I found my editor. I'm grateful for Pam helping me to keep taking baby steps and to stay on track.

My close friend and personal life coach, Diane Thibodeau, knows me well and can see right through me. She knew the reason I was writing this book better than I did. Whenever I talked about how so many women need this book and imagined the women it would help, she would remind me that the book was really for my healing journey. She would listen patiently to all my big plans and then say, "Remember, you're writing this for yourself." Her perspective and insight were such gifts to me, helping me stay grounded in the process and true to myself. Thank you, Diane.

Vicky Kirby, another good friend, helped me with the endless process of finding test readers. Every time I sent her a part of the book to read, she immediately responded with high praise. Her unwavering support and belief in me kept boosting my belief in myself. As an extrovert, Vicky's contact list is vast! Since I am an introvert, her ability to connect so genuinely with so many people amazes me. I'm forever grateful for Vicky and all her friends who gave me constructive feedback on those first few chapters.

Both of my children, Lucas Paquette and Michael Paquette, were great cheerleaders for me. They've known for many years I wanted to write a book and they've always had 100% faith in me. When I felt doubtful or confused during my writing process, they always had encouraging words for me, like: "Of course you can write a book." "You're an expert, Mom." "You'll help a lot of people." Thank you, Lucas and Michael, for having your mom's back!

~

Introduction

We are born with curiosity, sensitivity, and natural abilities and talents—inherently worthy of love and attention. Then our unique personality slowly fades as we armor our sensitive heart against hurt and pain. We grow into one big coping mechanism rather than our natural, brilliant, and complex selves. And we don't even realize it's happening. How and why did we lose ourselves?

Those of us who are highly sensitive take in more of the world than others. We have questions. We want explanations and clarification. We want to make sense of it all so our mind and body can rest. When we are children, we have no idea how to regulate our sensitivity as we are constantly bombarded with information. We only have our tiny child brain to figure things out and come up with answers. This is how the habits of overthinking, analyzing, and problem-solving start. In a near-constant state of being overwhelmed and without adequate answers or support from our parents, anxiety creeps in and stays.

Childhood Emotional Neglect

I truly believe there is a wide range of "normal." Some children are born highly sensitive while others seem resilient and capable from an early age. These variations are due to personality, temperament, parent/child fit, home environment, the emotional health of the parents, and the resilience of the child and parent. The pairing of a highly sensitive child with an emotionally insensitive parent is a perfect set up for childhood emotional neglect.

After many years of studying children's emotional health and many more years of personal healing, I have come to believe that most people have experienced some level of such neglect. We may not recall any particular traumatic event, but we instinctively know that some things didn't feel right. Childhood emotional neglect describes what was missing in our growing-up years, from warmth and nurturing to support and validation.

I didn't see my own childhood as traumatic until postpartum depression sent me to therapy in my thirties. Even then, I defended and made excuses for my parent's behavior and focused on the positive experiences. Until my fifties, I still wasn't able to see what my childhood was missing and how it affected me. I didn't connect the dots between my inability to feel and receive nurturing, comfort, kindness, and warmth from others and the lack of these emotions in my childhood. As opposed to childhood abuse where people can usually remember a specific event, this is the hidden injury of "childhood emotional neglect." Jonice Webb coined this term in her book, *Running on Empty*. She describes childhood emotional neglect as "an invisible force from your childhood which you can't see but may be affecting you profoundly to this day. It is about what didn't happen in your childhood, what wasn't said, and what cannot be remembered."

I've always felt a general kind of love for all people, wishing them the best. I never understood hate or meanness. But in my personal relationships, it has been difficult to feel love or to let my guard down. Trying to read expressions and decipher other's intentions and emotions to feel safe enough to interact in a loving way has not been easy. I would always feel vulnerable, unable to trust that people were truly genuine and kind, wary that they would be dismissive, mean, or rude. This chronic wariness and vulnerability were blocking my true feelings and distorting my natural abilities of sensitivity, empathy, and intuition.

Distorted Natural Abilities

Through my personal and professional experience, I have come to believe that if you are sensitive in one area—say, emotionally—you are also sensitive in other areas—such as mentally, physically, and psychically. I call these hyper-sensitivities "natural abilities" rather than deficits. All of the children I see in my practice are emotionally sensitive; many have physical sensitivities like allergies, asthma, and eczema or are unusually vulnerable to noise, touch, or smells. Some have sensory processing disorders or attention deficit disorders. Others are highly intuitive or even psychic.

Growing up in an emotionally dysfunctional family, our precious natural abilities become distorted and used as coping mechanisms. Sensitivity is twisted into behaviors of compliance to avoid punishment, arguments, or any type of conflict. Our natural intuition is re-directed to please others and anticipate their needs. True empathy turns into excess concern, chronic caretaking, and martyrdom. Natural mindfulness becomes hyper-vigilance—monitoring others for dysregulated emotions so we can neutralize them ahead of time.

Highly sensitive children become traumatized more easily than others. Yelling, bullying, unfairness, or meanness can put them on edge for hours or even days. When this happens over and over without relief, the anxiety becomes chronic. Without help from an adult, children have no resources. They don't have the cognitive ability to rationalize a parent's behavior. They take it personally. They haven't developed enough self-knowledge to know they don't deserve to be treated badly. So, they internalize ideas like, "Nobody likes me," "I'm not good enough," "I'm stupid," "I'm not lovable," "There's something wrong with me." These false beliefs come to dominate our thoughts, color our relationships, and diminish our overall success in life.

In an emotionally neglectful childhood, we develop an outside focus, monitoring and caring for others' wellbeing before our own, shaping our self-expression to fit another person's needs. These become survival mechanisms for what feels like a toxic environment. As adults, we will tend to underestimate our abilities and feel like we have to go above and beyond at all times. To feel worthy of even the slightest kindness or appreciation, we set high expectations for ourselves. To break these patterns and change our beliefs, we have to come to know ourselves through a different lens.

Our task, then, is to develop a new identity, a new idea of ourselves that reflects who we really are and who we were born to be. In this way, we will finally be able to claim our natural talents and abilities and use them in healthy ways, not as coping mechanisms. Essentially, we need to relearn how to live and love with our whole heart as our authentic selves.

Who This Book Is For

This book will break your heart and then help you mend it. It is for women, like you, on a path of personal development or spiritual growth who have come up against roadblocks and don't understand why they stalled out. Even with a dedicated mindset and persistent effort, it's difficult to cultivate and sustain a new perspective, behavior, or belief. They don't think to look back to their past for clues to hidden emotional wounding. Most women feel that they've had a good childhood and a good life, and their lives may look fine from the outside.

But these loving, capable, intelligent women aren't really fulfilled, and they don't know why, no matter how much effort they put into self-improvement. Like you, they want to be and do more in the world, but no self-help strategies have worked. Because they don't know enough about themselves at a deeper level, they are unable to create a life that reflects who they are. They feel hollow; relationships are shallow; work isn't satisfying.

The solution: turn your attention inward to discover the root of the problem. Dig down deep to see how your identity, wants, needs, and preferences were undeveloped or even buried in an emotionally stunting childhood. If you aren't aware that you experienced childhood emotional neglect, you will see yourself for the first time in this book. You will finally discover an explanation for your chronic discontent and why being better, nicer, and giving more hasn't helped. And then you will discover your true self.

> "Often it's the deepest pain which empowers you to grow into your highest self."
>
> —Karen Salmansohn, Founder, NotSalmon

About the Book

This book is about emotions. You will feel a full range of them as you read true stories from my own experiences as well as those of my clients (whose names and details have been changed to protect their privacy). In part 1, the Wounding section of the book, you will often see yourself in the children's stories, sometimes as the child and sometimes as the mother. In part 2, Coping, you will feel like a mirror is being held up to your adult self. There will be *Aha!* moments and tears. Hold on to your seat and keep going. Do what you need to support and be kind to yourself. Breathe. Notice the thoughts and emotions that come up. Write them down to explore later or just let them pass through. Part 3, the final section of the book, Healing, will give you everything you need to finally heal your emotional wounds. You will come to a new way of being, seeing, and feeling yourself, experiencing love in your heart for yourself and others.

> "Those who feel lovable, who love, and who experience belonging simply believe they are worthy of love and belonging."
>
> —Brené Brown, from *Daring Greatly*

If you have children, your thoughts may stray to the effects of your emotional wounds on them. As you read, I encourage you to stay with your own experience. Keep your focus on the memories, dreams, and emotions that come up for you. This is *your* healing journey, and it must be done first before trying to change your relationship or your behavior with your children.

In the Healing section of this book, I describe a combination of psychological and spiritual concepts, practices, and tools to facilitate true self-healing. They have been accumulated over many years of personal experience and fine-tuned in my counseling practice. Some I learned from educational trainings and conferences with the American Holistic Nurses Association, the HeartMath Institute, and the Integrative Healthcare Symposium. Others, I learned from a spiritual self-development program I participated in and then helped to develop and teach. Still others were developed by a psychic (since passed) who opened me up to new ideas and a bigger version of myself. The philosophies of yoga and over twenty years of yoga practice have been additionally influential.

I've also integrated concepts from the writings of Eckhart Tolle, Shakti Gawain, Don Miguel Ruiz, Gary Chapman, Brené Brown, Bruce Lipton, Gabor Maté, Thomas Hübl, and Jonice Webb. More recently, I've incorporated the latest approaches and strategies from life coach training with the Co-Active Training Institute. All of these practices have been tried and tested by my clients—mostly women and children—helping them to heal from chronic stress, anxiety, depression, attention-deficit/hyperactivity disorders (ADHD), and obsessive-compulsive disorders (OCD).

The pervasive idea in the wellness community that we must look to an expert for instruction on how to heal ourselves reminds me of the limiting beliefs and practices I experienced while working in traditional medicine. For my own healing, moving away from traditional medical treatments toward natural healthcare was the start of truly healing myself. But it wasn't until I added spiritual growth work that I felt exponential improvement in my well-being.

Go Deep to Fly High

If you were drawn to this book, it means you are ready for it. You have the strength and courage to heal your wounds. You are also, most likely, a highly sensitive person and possibly empathic or intuitive as well.

I believe our spirit was born into our family of origin for the purpose of honing these natural traits. There's a benefit from being exposed to difficult childhood circumstances, but only if you are willing to go through the challenging process of healing. The further you go into the depths of your emotions, the higher you will rise on your spiritual journey.

Our soul sets an intention for our life before we are born, and it chooses our family to help us learn the lessons we need for our soul's growth. And so, a piece of our soul incarnates on earth to have a particular human experience. I call this piece the "higher self." Our higher self holds all the wisdom we've accumulated over many lifetimes. We can learn to draw guidance from this higher, wiser self anytime we need it. You only need to get quiet, ask for help, and then listen.

> "She could never go back and make some of the details pretty. All she could do was move forward and make the whole beautiful."
>
> —Terri St. Cloud, Founder, Bone Sigh Arts

— Part 1 —

Wounding: Experience of Emotional Neglect in Childhood

~

CHAPTER 1

The Forgotten Child

When children's needs for comfort, care, and support are neglected, they can feel forgotten—neither considered nor acknowledged. They don't know why this is happening, but they feel something is wrong. They sense the discrepancy between an innate knowledge of their worthiness and how seldom it is recognized. Their natural talents, like sensitivity and empathy, can be taken advantage of, ignored, and even disparaged. As children continue to live with this uncertainty, they become anxious, shy, and vigilant. When a child's unique interests and desires aren't nurtured, they become sad, depressed, and angry. A common way that children are forgotten is when, for whatever reason, they are put into a caretaker role in their family. They end up feeling overly responsible for the well-being of others despite having no skills or preparation. Not surprisingly, they start to feel inadequate. They can also develop deep feelings of insecurity because no one is parenting *them*.

In the following stories, you may recognize some patterns that happened in *your* family. If your parent suffered from drug or alcohol addiction, mental illness, anger issues, or was emotionally or physically absent, it's likely you assumed you weren't worthy of their attention. There are two ways children generally cope with this: by becoming cooperative, quiet, and helpful, or fighting for attention with angry outbursts. As an adult, you may still be fitting in or fighting to be acknowledged while often feeling uncertain, unseen, unsupported, and insecure. Your adult habits of people-pleasing and caretaking others' emotions stem from this feeling of unworthiness in childhood. As you will see below and in subsequent chapters, some of the stories are from my personal experiences and some I've heard from child clients in my counseling practice.

Uncertain

My anxiety likely started in my mother's womb. My first memory of it happened when I was five years old. I was on my way to the first day of kindergarten in the back of my neighbor's station wagon. I wasn't nervous to leave home or start school; I was nervous about leaving my mother alone. I really believed she couldn't take care of my three-year-old sister on her own. I was "parentified" or "adultified"—when a child takes on the role of a parent—at a very young age. A psychic once told me I started taking care of my mother from the cradle. I don't *really* know what she meant by that, but I imagine I was adjusting my energy and adapting my expectations to her moods.

My mother had mental illness when I was young but never had a formal diagnosis or treatment. Back in the 1960s, she was labeled a "nervous housewife" and prescribed amphetamines to get up in the morning and benzodiazepines to sleep at night. There was very little known about mental illness back then, especially by our small-town general practitioner. So, as the oldest child—but still a small, thin, pale, highly sensitive little girl—I did everything I could to get her through each day. I never wondered, "Where is my father, my aunt, my grandmother?" I just assumed she was my responsibility, and there was no one around to help me think otherwise.

I became ever vigilant, watching her face, body, and movements for clues to her mood, trying to anticipate the next thing that would make her blow up or break down. Occasionally I would think, *Why is she using me, disregarding my needs?* I know now that I didn't deserve it, that her treatment of me was based on her illness, not my worthiness. But I sure worked hard to gain her love or even just some positive attention. Later in life, I talked with my aunt about how she saw the situation. She said my mother treated me like a slave. This is a different kind of trauma than physical abuse. This is emotional neglect.

And so, anxiety was wired into my body from birth. What I didn't know then was how much it would affect my physical, mental, and emotional health for the rest of my life. I rarely played outside with other children. Whenever I joined my middle sister and the neighborhood kids as they rode their bikes, built forts, and climbed trees—feeling so carefree—I would inevitably be called back to the house to help my mother care for my littlest sister. I never did feel like "one of the kids." From this experience and many others like it, I developed social anxiety with thoughts like, "No one likes me" and "They've left me behind again," feeling rejected before I even knew how to socialize.

I came to prefer being around adults. What little attention I got was praise for being mature, smart, responsible, and capable—an identity that was decided for me and that I efficiently took on. I had learned to come when called, be agreeable, obey, anticipate problems, and solve them. I played the role of caretaker so others could be free from my mother's rages, crying jags, and unpredictable moods. Looking back now as an adult, the praise I received served to keep me in my place.

Things did improve over time, but not much. My mother became more stable when I was in middle school and high school, but the damage was already done. My early childhood was bootcamp for an adolescence filled with insecurity, low self-esteem, social anxiety, self-consciousness, and loneliness. I was still consumed with being good, doing the right thing, getting good grades, and avoiding offending my mother in any way. I had to come home every day after school and watch soap operas with her to keep her company. The only acceptable reason to leave her was homework, which became my code word to escape even when there was no homework to do. If I did anything wrong, contradicted her, or made a suggestion, she took it personally—crying, complaining, yelling, or pouting. My habit of vigilance was still in full force.

Unseen

Going back as far as I can remember—sometime around three years old—there is a slip of memory of my father and I looking at the stars. He was naming the constellations, pointing them out in the dark sky. It was thrilling and special. When I asked him what was beyond the stars, he didn't have an answer. *But there has to be something!* I thought. *How can you not know?* This was the first of many philosophical questions I posed during my childhood. Being generally met with inadequate responses, I always felt let down, defeated in my quest for knowledge. I assumed that when I grew up and became an adult, I would finally know everything. Another disappointment to come.

Although there was no internet in the 1960s and '70s, we did have a set of the *World Book Encyclopedia*, but I always wanted to know more, such as how people were feeling and how things affected them. Not just the facts. Unfortunately, there was never an emphasis on learning at home; my parents didn't think it was important. My questions were brushed off as trivial and unnecessary. So, I buried myself in books but was hard-pressed to find anything compelling or meaningful in what was available to me.

In early childhood, it's necessary for children to align themselves with their parents to feel emotionally secure. It's an unconscious process of forming an identity to fit the surrounding emotional climate. But it's also important to maintain some sense of individuality. For example, when a child's natural talents aren't acknowledged or nurtured, she loses a piece of herself. I never really lost my curiosity and quest for knowledge, but I did have to tolerate my parents continued indifference. I had to keep pushing for more homework time or to take higher-level classes. They would try to talk me out of it and rarely saw my side. Something I was excited about and felt was important was constantly disparaged. It was another form of childhood emotional neglect.

Because I have these wounds, I am acutely aware of them in my clients. I see it in children, and I see it in their mothers. I see it passed down through ideas, beliefs, and behaviors. I just want to hug all the kids and tell the moms they are doing a great job. Because they are, as much as they are able. But most importantly, we spend our time unraveling the dynamic between mother and child.

Unsupported

Jill wants to fly airplanes. She's fifteen years old, a sweet and serious girl, but antisocial and depressed. She has little interest in discussing her needs. *What is missing in your life?* "I want to learn to fly." *Have you taken driving lessons?* "No, I don't care about driving." Jill's mother is worried about her low mood, crankiness, not fitting in with peers, *and* her preoccupation with planes. She wants her on the "right path," able to socialize, do well in school, and prepare for college. She wants me to fix her, to help her squeeze into a box that would make the mother comfortable so she can breathe easier.

Jill just wants to be Jill, in all her weirdness, but she's feeling unsupported and unacceptable in her family. She sits on my couch and insists that flying planes will make everything better. This is her passion, and she is longing to pursue it. Jill has done all the research to get started, but she needs her mother's help. Will she support Jill's dreams or let her own doubts and worries steer Jill's course? My recommendation to her mother: Get this kid in a plane!

In an alternate, more conventional scenario, the child would be prescribed antidepressants and goals would be set for her that reflect her mother's idea of an appropriate life. As for the happiness, support, and love the child deserves to experience, they get buried under the mother's insecurity. The child's passions are quashed because they feel too risky for the mother.

Fortunately, Jill's mom did step up and found a way to get her flying lessons. A few years later, I saw Jill again after her first year of college, where she was majoring in aviation science. She was still the same person: direct, serious, and caring little about what other people thought of her. Living with a roommate was distracting Jill from her studies, and she was feeling anxious about not doing well academically. But all she needed were a few organizational tools and a letter stating she required a single dorm room.

Insecure

I remember enjoying the beach one day with a friend when a frustrating situation caught my eye. A young girl, not quite a teen, was trying to corral her younger siblings and bring them out of the water. I watched her failed attempts to get her little brother to follow directions. The parents were sitting behind and to the right of me and I could hear them asking the kids to get out of the water. Their tone wasn't urgent, but they did keep repeating it.

The older sibling—the young girl—was trying to mind the parents and get her younger siblings to do the same. She was having particular trouble with the little boy, probably around two. She would grab him and then he would wiggle out of her arms and run back in the water, laughing. It was all a game to him. He felt no urgency to mind the parents. The young girl, however, was getting desperate. Every time the boy slipped her grasp, she looked imploringly at the parents for help. I watched the scene for several minutes as she tried at least five more times to get her little brother, looking back at her parents each time. My heart went out to this young girl as her pain was very familiar. She was expected, without any instruction or help, to manage her younger siblings.

I was also noticing my reaction to this scene. I was on the edge of my seat, completely connected with the girl. I felt the desperation and the sense of being overwhelmed in her silent plea for help, and her frustration, sadness, and disbelief that her parents would let this continue. It was difficult for me not to intervene. Finally, the father walked down to the water and helped get the younger kids out. There was no comforting of the young girl, no thank you, no praise for trying to help. As the father managed the siblings without so much as a glance at the girl, she stood there looking relieved but also forlorn. Her emotional needs had been completely neglected and now she was forgotten again. She was on her own to calm her nervous system and make sense of the situation.

Her thoughts most likely focused on blaming herself for failing her parents again. As a child, she doesn't have the maturity or experience to understand that she deserves to be treated like one of the children, not an adult. In situations like this, she will always fail because she expects herself to fulfill a role that is too big for her.

A Holistic Healing Process

As an adult, you may still (like me) be over-caring for others, fighting to be seen like Jill, and/or unable to ask for help like the girl on the beach. To soothe your feelings of insecurity, uncertainty, and unworthiness, you need to shift your focus to yourself. And as an adult *woman*, it can be especially difficult to put yourself first with all your responsibilities and obligations. But guess what? You—and only you—are responsible for your own well-being. Others are responsible for theirs. It's important that you experience meeting your own needs first and take action on your own behalf. This behavior change will be the start of believing in your own worthiness. And you cannot truly be there for others if you are depleted and haven't taken care of yourself.

The following process of building self-awareness will help you discover and unravel false beliefs, distorted thought patterns, and harmful behaviors. By taking ownership of your daily energy level and mood, you will begin to shift to new thoughts, beliefs, and behaviors.

> "When I own my stuff and am conscious of my own interior, then I am a partner of the world, not a helper of the world. I am a partner in a co-creative process."
>
> —Thomas Hübl, 9/1/2020, *Why You Shouldn't Try to "Help" Others, Here's What to Do Instead,* *eomega.org*

Daily Awareness Practice

- **Allow** yourself time and space for underlying emotions and feelings to surface such as sadness, resentment, exhaustion, or feeling taken advantage of.

- **Acknowledge** these emotions and feelings as they come up without self-judgment or making up a story about them. They are all valid.

- **Accept** your current state of being, sit with the sensations, and claim them as your own to feel and heal. Avoid negative *or* positive labels and don't blame others.

Notice what you want to do differently, such as carving out time for relaxation, or prioritize for saying no when you are depleted. Write about what you discover and what you plan to do.

Take one action per day; baby steps are the best way to get to where you want to go. And don't forget to pat yourself on the back! Repeat daily.

~

CHAPTER 2

The Highly Sensitive Child

An emotionally insensitive or immature parent, paired with an emotionally sensitive child, leaves both parties struggling to understand each other. This makes for a stressful household on top of everyday pressures like work, school, and other responsibilities. Because they need extra emotional support, these children are always at a deficit, looking for comfort and security from parents who are unable to provide it. To maintain a balanced nervous system, they create maladaptive coping skills. You know you were a sensitive child if you were frequently told to calm down, stop crying, stop yelling, or sit down. Your emotions were too big or too deep for your parents to manage.

Over time, you are likely to have become distrustful, ashamed, easily overwhelmed, or angry. As an adult, you may be carrying these feelings around without being aware of it. These feelings shaped your beliefs about yourself and the world. If you have over-arching beliefs like, "People are hurtful," "You can't trust anyone," "No one understands me," or "There is something wrong with me," then it's very likely you are a highly sensitive person who experienced emotional neglect as a child. See if you recognize your childhood experiences in the following stories.

Distrustful

One night my mother was tucking me into bed with a smile on her face and uncertainty in her eyes. "Doesn't that feel nice to be all clean and cozy in your pajamas?" she asked as she leaned over me. However, her words and facial expression didn't match what I felt from her, which was uneasiness and insecurity, as if she was hoping my answer would validate her as a good mother. I was alert, wary, trying to figure out the appropriate response. I knew if my answer was "wrong," every-thing would change for the worse, from pouting to an angry blow-up. I knew this from experience. It often happened when something didn't work out: the dinner was burned or the car wouldn't start. She would sud-denly become irritated, disappointed, or overwhelmed with emotion. My sisters and I were never helpful or grateful enough to satisfy her insecurity.

Even at a very early age, I was acutely aware of both my own emotions and those of others. Being highly sensitive and empathetic, I always recognized any disconnect between what people expressed and their true emotions. So, this bedtime routine didn't feel like the loving gesture that was intended. My emotional need for a warm, comforting goodnight wasn't met, replaced instead with distrust and an emotional instinct to care-take my mother. When young children experience ongoing distrust of a parent, the attachment bond will, over time, break or may never develop. It feels like being thrown into the air without a net, and if there is a net, it's one with holes in it. The worst part is the lack of consistency, making it impossible to ever feel safe. I was too young to predict whether or not my needs would be met. Looking back, it felt like being forced into war as a young, inexperienced soldier, not knowing where the bombs were buried and without a captain to lead me through the minefield.

Ashamed

Ellie is an easy-going seven-year-old, but around her mom she is nervous. She's never quite sure what her mom wants from her. Ellie has ADHD and anxiety, so she is active with a short attention span and overly sensitive to noise, chaos, and confusion. Her little brother, on the other hand, loves noise and being in charge of things. Ellie always wants to play with her brother (it's hard for her to play alone), but she hates that her brother always takes the lead. The result: They fight every day. Ellie's mother feels her behavior is wrong and must be stopped, and that it's Ellie's fault because she is older. Every day mom scolds her: "Ellie, you can't do that! It's wrong to yell at your brother." Mom is exasperated that Ellie continues to repeat the behavior. Her message of right and wrong is not getting through. While her mom and I talk about this, Ellie is usually rolling on the floor of my office looking sad. When asked about the situation, Ellie blames her brother and says that *his* behavior is wrong.

This is the dilemma of blaming and shaming. Ellie, being so sensitive, can't really hear what her mother is saying when she is being shamed. She is consumed with thinking she must be a bad kid, unworthy of her parent's love. "Shame is so painful for children because it is inextricably linked to the fear of being unlovable," says Brené Brown in her book, *Daring Greatly*. "For young children who are still dependent on their parents for survival—for food, shelter, and safety— feeling unlovable is a threat to survival. It's trauma." After the shame comes sadness and anger as Ellie points the finger at her brother to share the pain and deflect her hurt feelings. She is looking for a parent to soothe her and help her manage her irritation and overwhelm. Her need in this moment is to feel supported, cared for, and seen for who she is. Her high sensitivity must be addressed first. Then, when she feels supported, Ellie will be ready to listen and make efforts to cooperate.

Overwhelmed

One night when I was around eight, I remember watching the news with my parents and seeing a video of emaciated, starving children drinking from puddles. I was astonished, heartbroken, and angry. How could this be happening in the world!? I felt helpless and couldn't imagine why the adults in charge weren't fixing this right away. What a horrible world to live in where it wasn't a priority to make sure children got fed. And so, I had lots of questions. My parents' answers, unfortunately, were off-hand and weak, as if this was something we just had to accept.

As noted above, highly sensitive and empathic children are constantly attuned to the emotions of others—whether in person or from images on TV. These feelings are overwhelming most of the time and terrifying some of the time. They simply don't have the cognitive ability to see the bigger picture. If our parents are emotionally immature or self-absorbed, such children don't get the attention, explanations, or comfort they need and end up feeling abandoned and defeated.

My sisters and I played with our male cousins regularly and the boys often got into fights. I could never understand why people would hurt each other. Just witnessing bullying broke my heart. When they beat each other up, my nervous system exploded. I never saw the end of a fight because I had to walk away and block my ears. My aunt would yell from inside the house, "Love one another!" I was so angry because she wouldn't come out and solve the problem like I thought adults were supposed to do.

Did the adults around me even notice my sensitivity? If they did (and through no fault of their own), they were likely too ill-equipped to help. I know they cared, but in a detached way: "Let the kids solve their own problems." This is the opposite of what children need. In such situations, they long for thoughtful and helpful support from adults. Children count on parents to navigate stressful situations, to nurture, teach, and support them through difficult times. It was clear that my distress was not a priority for my parents; it wasn't even on their radar. I learned to handle it myself and even hide it for fear of being disparaged. But to give up expecting support from your parents is a deep loss.

Some children don't give up so easily. Their sensitivity shows up as anger, yelling, hitting, or throwing things to attract their parent's attention. This is a desperate bid for connection. Underneath the anger is a history of frustration and disappointment. All they want is to feel a loving, caring connection with their parents. Like Ellie in the previous story and Caitlyn in the next one, they just want their emotional needs met.

Angry

Caitlyn complains about her parents: "They don't listen. They just tell me what to do." She is high spirited, insistent, and argumentative. As a fourteen-year-old with high expectations of herself, she needs support from her parents to manage her busy life. Her parents respond with, "She doesn't listen. She interrupts and pushes her own agenda." Caitlyn is highly sensitive and takes everything personally. She's intense, creative, and disorganized, easily overwhelmed and emotionally reactive. If the slightest thing doesn't go her way, it triggers her insecurity and she breaks down into crying or yelling. She and her parents fight almost daily, which has contributed to Caitlyn's anxiety and depression. To feel emotionally stable, she needs daily contact with her friends. And when her parents take her phone away as punishment for her uncooperative behavior, it's devastating. She feels her parents are being unnecessarily mean—or worse.

Given Caitlyn's temperament, her parents feel it's important to tightly manage her grades, schedule, and activities, reminding her several times a day what she needs to do and when. This drives Caitlyn crazy! They are afraid she will fail a class, be unprepared for her acting roles (she loves theater), or get behind on her chores. This constant monitoring is driven by her parents' fear and anxiety, perpetuating the divide between them and their daughter. Caitlyn's feelings of inadequacy and insecurity are heightened by her parent's behavior. Their well-intentioned support is eroding Caitlyn's self-worth.

After a year of counseling, Caitlyn's parents began to soften their approach, learning to understand the emotional needs of their daughter and how to best support her. Caitlyn's mother was willing to look at her own anxiety, and both parents learned to connect with Caitlyn lovingly, patiently, and authentically. Caitlyn and her parents are practicing their communication skills: avoiding reactivity, taking breaks to balance their emotions, slowing down the conversation, asking questions for clarification, negotiating, focusing on what's going right, and respecting individual differences and boundaries. Caitlyn is already saying that she feels more supported, confident, and capable. The true benefit of this mutual communication is that Caitlyn feels held, seen, and heard by her parents.

A Holistic Healing Process

As a highly sensitive adult woman, you may feel like no one values the assets you bring to the table such as creativity (like Caitlyn), sensing other's emotions (like me), showing empathy, or communication skills. You may not feel like such abilities are valuable because you've been shamed like Ellie. Certainly, there are plenty of cultural messages that say showing emotion is weak and taking action is more powerful than talking. So how can you start to value your abilities, manage your sensitivity, and care for yourself? Here is a simple practice to use when you are feeling overwhelmed with sensory input or your own emotions. It only takes a few minutes, and you can use it anywhere to reconnect with yourself and recharge.

Grounding Visualization

"My body is my home. The earth is my charging station."

- Sit down, get comfortable and still, take a few deep breaths, and close your eyes.

- Feel your feet on the floor and imagine energy coming up from the ground through your body.

- Now imagine pulling all your energy in from the environment around you: the people, the situations, the noise and distractions.

- Move your focus from your thoughts and into your body.

- Notice your breathing as you continue to imagine stabilizing earth energy coming up through you and all your outside energy coming back into you.

- Feel a sense of the clear, calm energy available to you.

- Open your eyes when you feel relaxed and recharged.

~

CHAPTER 3

The Lost Child

A child's personality and identity can become distorted, lost, or never developed due to emotional wounding. When they are expected to conform and comply, a child's true identity isn't nurtured into being. Girls, especially, may take on an unassuming, helpful personality as a survival mechanism to avoid hurtful interactions. Disengagement from life is the next level of shrinking themselves. Without support and validation of their budding personality from their parents, children can become indecisive, morphing their personality to adapt to the situation, never considering or even knowing their own personal preferences. At this stage, the child becomes discouraged and gives up hope. This is when depression can develop. Because she is unable to ask for what she needs, the child experiences her struggles alone. This feels intuitively wrong and sad, but she knows no other way.

You may recognize yourself as a lost child as you read the following stories. You may have come to believe that being cooperative, compliant, and flexible are some of your assets. You smooth things over by sensing everyone else's needs and not considering yours as part of the equation. If this is so, you were trained as a child to take yourself out of your own life. You may be longing for connection, but it feels impossible because you aren't connected to your own true identity. It's buried under the survival personality you unconsciously created.

Compliance

One day when I was around ten, I was in a hula-hoop contest at my local playground. This was an end-of-summer event where all the playgrounds in town joined together to play games and compete. I had made it to the final round with one other girl. There wasn't much glory in my life, so this was special. I knew I could hula-hoop forever! We were going on twenty minutes or so when my mother came to pick me up. She had not come to watch me or cheer me on and I hadn't expected it. She honked and yelled from the car that I had to come now. I think I asked her to wait, but she insisted. I was having a rare moment of freedom and fun—feeling so confident and the center of attention. I forfeited the competition to go shopping with her.

Disobeying my mother was unthinkable. She would have come out of the car, yelling. I can picture her as I write this: angry, insistent, not a single thought about my disappointment or what I wanted in that moment. No compromise, no awareness of the situation, no flexibility; just escalating emotions until I complied.

Patterns of persistent compliance lead to feeling misunderstood, unseen, or not valued. It is the opposite of that warm feeling of belonging. From a young age, there is a deep knowing that there must be more to life than doing what you're told and trying to be who others need you to be: The good child, the babysitter, the listening ear, the talented child, the smart child, to name just a few. Compliance feels like acting out a required persona while constantly wondering if you're getting it right. You feel unsure at every turn, re-evaluating situations to adapt to what is needed. The ability to think, behave, and feel like your true self is lost when compliance is required. There is no rebellion or resistance, just chronic anxiety.

This leads to a cycle of trying to be better and even *more* capable to alleviate that anxiety: more quiet and polite and cooperative, ready to help at any moment. Never asking for your own needs and wants to be considered. Never asserting your opinion. You remain stuck in your prescribed role so that others don't have to look at or change their behavior. The emotional atmosphere in the household is constantly uncomfortable. This is how Laurie, in the next story, felt about her home environment. She was never quite at ease enough to try new things or ask for help, which significantly delayed her development.

Disengagement

The first thing that comes to my mind when I think of Laurie are the words, "I don't know." Over the past two years, this has been the answer to most questions at her counseling appointments. "What's important to you?" I would ask. "What would you like more of in your life? Who can help you? How can you get started?" She has tremendous difficulty deciphering how she feels, what she wants, what she likes, or what she's good at. She doesn't know what the problem is, how to get help, or who can help. She is off her path without a firm identity. She is lost.

Laurie is sixteen years old with the diagnoses of depression, anxiety, and gastritis. It shows up as boredom, inertia, indecisiveness, stomach pains, social anxiety, and agoraphobia. She is paralyzed by fuzzy thinking, low mood, low engagement in life, and an inability to commit to anything, Laurie often feels helpless and hopeless. Her parents go through cycles of wanting to help, then become annoyed and frustrated. "Why can't she just do the things she is supposed to do—get good grades, make friends, go out to restaurants?" There is little warmth in their relationship, only praise for new behaviors and actions. Instead of empathy, patience, and reassurance, Laurie's parents issue directives with a dose of disappointment and exasperation.

In one session, Laurie became more animated about doing her artwork. She told me about her ideas for sketches and new techniques she wants to try. I was surprised that she felt this comfortable revealing her true self. I became excited, too! I mirrored this excitement back to her for fear it would quickly fade. We discussed her ideas, and I made every effort to validate her as a person, an artist, and a creator. Unfortunately, this turned out to be a one-time episode; she was back to silent inertia at her next session. Without encouragement from her parents, Laurie's hopefulness is fleeting. If she hasn't been supported in her true self-expression, she will always crave her parents' validation, approval, and love no matter how old she is or what she has to give up to get them. Such neglect can start from birth. When emotional needs are ignored in infancy, a child automatically adapts by either shutting down—less crying, less eye contact, less verbalizing— or escalating: more crying, flailing limbs, inconsolable. Their natural temperament, the one they are born with, is suppressed.

Depression

At sixteen, I had my first experience with depression. I was still playing the role of caretaker and good girl. I had not developed any hobbies or skills to round out my identity. Because my mother wanted me home with her, I wasn't allowed to stay after school for activities. I was socially inept. My true identity was underdeveloped, buried under my prescribed role in the family.

The depression started when close friends began dropping me and I had no prospects for a boyfriend. Since I was good at watching others, I could copy appropriate social behavior, but there was no feeling behind it. I never felt close to my peers. I was consumed with feeling sorry for myself that they didn't like me. I cried alone at night in my bed, never thinking to seek comfort from my parents. I felt they didn't care enough to hear about my problems. My mother's problems were always top priority in our household.

The straw that put me over the edge into depression was when my parents told me I wouldn't be going to college. I had been secretly thinking that college was the only way out of my caretaker role in the family. They said there was no money for that. None of my family members on either side had gone to college; it just wasn't something we did. I was stunned. I felt like a big trick had been played on me. I was in the top 15% of my graduating class and my peers were going to Ivy League colleges.

When I stopped talking and refused to go to school, I was taken to the doctor. I invented a sore throat. The doctor tested me for mononucleosis and said it was negative but that I was "a very sick girl." That was the extent of any diagnosis or treatment. I was allowed to stay home for a week. During that week, I came to realize I was on my own to figure out a way to move forward. I felt completely alone. It never occurred to me to ask a teacher or a relative for support.

One night, I was writhing in my bed, crying, feeling lost, with no understanding of what was happening. Why am I not loved? Why doesn't anyone have answers to my questions? About God, Jesus, the world, my place in it? Am I like Jesus? Am I that different, that special? What am I supposed to do? Why isn't God helping me feel better? How does God help people? All of a sudden, an answer popped into my head: "Through your hands, I work through you." I tried to make sense of this message with the limited knowledge and words I had for spirituality, universal intelligence, higher self—whatever you prefer to call it. The understanding I came to was this: God works *through* me, not for me. It meant that I had to take action.

Underneath all the despair, I had a deep but subtle knowing that I was worthy of love and was bewildered to feel so invisible to those around me. I truly wanted to be my best self at all times. I cared for people. I had great sensitivity to others' emotions and problems. I just knew there was a bigger, better life out there for me. I had to decide: Am I going to jump out this second-story window (which wouldn't have killed me anyway), or am I going to find a way to leave this house and do whatever it takes to get to college?

Looking back, I was one of the kids who got lost, who fell through the cracks. I was dressed well, my parents acted normally, and I was well-behaved, so other adults had no idea that I needed help. I, too, remained under the illusion that I had a normal childhood until I started therapy in middle adulthood.

A Holistic Healing Process

Do you have trouble with depression or feeling disengaged from life? If yes, think about how often you had to comply as a child by assessing your environment and morphing into what was needed in the moment. As an adult woman, you may not know much about yourself: your likes and dislikes, how you feel, your real opinions. You may describe yourself in relation to others—caring, supportive, flexible—rather than focusing on your own personal attributes. Your overdeveloped sensitivity and empathy for others allows you to see all sides of an issue, but you hesitate to express your unique viewpoint. You may not even know your own viewpoint. As an adult, you may feel different from others, unable to trust or connect with them or yourself.

At a young age, your brain was wired to scan for emotionally unsafe situations and adapt your self-expression as quickly as possible. For the lost child, this results in confusing emotions and perceptions of yourself and the world.

> "As a child, your mind is in a lower vibrational state, theta, imagination. You copy what you see and hear and believe it's the truth about you and the world. The only way to override the program and believe something different is repetition. Daily practices of saying and doing something different is required."
>
> —Bruce H. Lipton, *The Biology of Belief: Unleashing the Power of Consciousness, Matter and Miracles*

The following is a healing process to use whenever you feel confused or disconnected. As you practice, you will begin to discover more about yourself. This process can get emotional. Sadness may come up when you realize how much and how often you deny your own wants and needs. Remember, this was an unconscious, adaptive process that was necessary in your childhood. To keep wearing your "acceptable mask," you had to bury yourself. It is now time for your full self to emerge. Self-knowledge is the first step to diving into the complexity and wonder of your true self. Doing so will allow you to enjoy and express your unique identity and personality.

Assets List

1. As you go through your day, start noticing what you are good at and what you enjoy.

2. Avoid focusing on what you do for others or how you make them feel. Keep your focus on your own feelings and what you are experiencing in each moment.

3. Every evening, write down a few things you noticed from the day. Include even the smallest things that felt good, like talking to a friend, finishing a work project, or eating delicious food.

4. Make a second column and write down corresponding assets you possess that made those experiences enjoyable. What is it in you that is able to appreciate those things? For example, if you really enjoyed your lunch, your asset may be Food Connoisseur!

If something feels enjoyable, easy, or natural for you, it's an asset. As you build your asset list, you are describing yourself in a new way. You are moving away from morphing yourself into how you *should* be, think, feel, or behave according to your childhood programming and toward how you *really* are, think, feel, and behave. Instead of defining yourself by how you improve other people's lives, you can now discover all of your own personality traits—strengths and talents to enjoy for yourself, to enhance your life. The person you were born to be will become clear to you. No one was born to serve others. We are here to co-create the world we desire *with* each other, adding our own unique talents equally to the mix.

~

CHAPTER 4

The Lonely Child

As the emotionally neglected child grows and moves into her adolescent years (twelve to eighteen), she develops a new set of problems. This is naturally a challenging time for any teen, who is now managing hormonal, emotional, and social changes. But years of emotional neglect have caused her to armor her heart, become highly self-reliant, and distrust people's motives. Because she didn't experience a warm, loving, supportive relationship with her parents, it's impossible for her to feel secure in her peer relationships. She understands the world better than most but doesn't know how to function in it. She is spending less and less time with her family and may have given up on a meaningful connection with her parents. In its place, she looks to her peer group for validation of her worthiness. But friendships with peers are inherently unreliable. Alliances change on a whim and the lonely, socially awkward, insecure child cannot keep up, causing a string of hurtful interactions. In her book, *Daring Greatly*, Brené Brown says, "We are hardwired to connect with others, it's what gives purpose and meaning to our lives, and without it, there is suffering."

The loneliness of adolescent years is especially disheartening. Misunderstood, unseen or unheard by both parents and peers, the child crawls into her own world, maybe leaving a crack open in the door. Do you remember feeling insecure about your relationships during these years—constantly wondering who likes you and who doesn't, if you're popular or at least noticeable? Did you spend your time obsessing over a potential relationship with someone you admired from afar or counting your likes on social media? Feeling detached from your family, anxious around your peers, and spending lots of time in your room were also signs that you were a lonely child. Did you think that this was normal adolescent behavior? It may have been common, but it's not emotionally healthy. It's a reaction to being hurt in many ways over many years.

Now, as an adult woman, you may still feel socially awkward, suffer from obsessive thinking, or tend to feel detached from people. If you are highly sensitive and empathetic, you may truly feel deeply for others but still have trouble making connections. Experiencing deep feelings and being unable to express them appropriately in social situations feels highly frustrating.

Low self-worth due to childhood emotional neglect is the cause of multiple social problems like poor communication skills, self-consciousness, people pleasing, devaluing your own ideas and opinions, and crippling fears of judgment, rejection, or bullying. See if the following stories spark memories of how you were hurt and how it shaped your social ability.

Awkward

Anna is highly sensitive, insightful, imaginative, and passionate about making the world a better place through political activism. She is sixteen years old with the diagnoses of depression and anxiety. Anna's sensitivity causes her to easily feel slighted and ignored and unworthy of the kids she admires, making it hard for her to connect with her peers. Because she experienced constant criticism (intended as motivation) about her body and her abilities from her family, she has poor body image and low self-worth. Anna spends a lot of time wishing she was prettier and that people were kinder. She keeps trying to make social connections but feels nervous, awkward, and self-conscious. She asks me what to write in a text so she sounds cool and confident, and then how to not be disappointed when her friend doesn't answer. Because Anna feels things deeply, she is looking for much more in a relationship than what most teenagers can give. She desperately wants someone to "see her" and give her the love and warmth that wasn't available in her childhood.

Over the years I counseled Anna, it became clear how stuck she was. She didn't dare express interest in her peers for fear of rejection, but she continued to long for meaningful peer relationships. We talked a lot about how all teens are insecure in some way and that everyone else did not have it all together like she thought they did. I encouraged her to practice connecting with her peers more casually and frequently but without attachment to an outcome. Anna's communication skills were so awkward that when she made small attempts to reach out to a potential friend, she would negate her own request by saying something like, "It's okay if you're busy." By highlighting her low self-worth, she sabotaged her efforts and was not successful.

Obsessed

Emotional neglect in Karen's childhood led to angry outbursts to get her parents' attention and validation. She needed more emotional connection than her parents were able to provide during their divorce. When these didn't work, she lost her trust in them and everyone else. Karen also experienced frustration with schoolwork due to executive functioning disorder—difficulty with memory, concentration, and organization. She received academic support but no emotional support. Instead, she felt pressured to do well academically and in dance performances. Whenever Karen had an experience she perceived as unfair or mean, she took it personally. Her emotions would escalate as if someone was poking at an open wound. She easily felt disrespected or attacked and blamed others for her discomfort. This behavior hurt her relationships and endeavors.

At eighteen years old, Karen is still emotionally volatile, going from sadness to anger to silent rage and then isolating herself to avoid more pain. She looks to her friendships to help her feel safe and admits that she's a people pleaser. Like many adolescent girls I see in my practice, she latches on to romantic relationships to boost her self-worth. She puts her heart and soul into romances, making them more meaningful than they really are. Karen lives in a fantasy world, obsessed with clues to how much her boyfriend loves her. Her inability to trust people keeps her constantly nervous and needing reassurance. Unfortunately, because of this insecurity, she attracts untrustworthy people. When Karen's latest boyfriend broke up with her, she was devastated, feeling worthless again. The incident sent her into a depression that included obsessing over why the relationship broke up. Was he with someone else? Should she block him on social media? Her inability to function without at least the illusion of love in her life leaves her vulnerable and emotionally fragile. After several counseling sessions, it is still difficult for her to let go of obsessive thoughts and focus on her own healing.

Detached

During my adolescent years, I felt like there must be something about me that was undesirable, but I was unable to figure it out. Sometimes I had friends, and sometimes I didn't. I felt like I was playing catch-up all the time, trying to understand what behavior would bring me social success. After several failed attempts to connect with others in my early teens, I developed habits that kept me away from people, avoiding the hurt of being ignored or rejected. I read books for entertainment. I told my parents I had homework so I could stay home from family gatherings. My free time was filled with work, studying, and TV. I had my routines, responsibilities, and goals—completely self-reliant in creating my life experience, trusting no one to exchange ideas with or confide in. I was in my own little cocoon of safety—bored and detached, with limited self-expression, squeezed tight as if I was wrapped in gauze, my view of the outside world hazy and diffuse. But there was always the feeling of something missing.

Still, I thought I was doing all the right things and that people should like me just because I was a good person. I truly didn't think I had to make an effort to get to know people, and it seemed impossible anyway. I was uninterested in most people and felt little curiosity or attraction that might have motivated me to make a connection. Occasionally, I felt a flicker of interest in someone, but I would admire them without interacting with them. I believed that I wasn't good enough to be their friend, that they would never like me or even notice me. I was too shy to speak to them first. Trapped in insecurity, unable to act, I would make up stories about why such relationships were hopeless, such as, "They already have enough friends." Feeling lonely, detached, and numb throughout my teen years, I was convinced it was all my fault that relationships were hard and unfulfilling. Because of emotional neglect in my childhood, I didn't know how to give and receive in a relationship and I didn't dare to try.

A Holistic Healing Process

Do you relate to any of these stories? Maybe you were socially awkward or obsessed with romance in your teen years. Possibly you were detached in other ways or even avoided people due to anxiety or sadness. Did you give up on receiving support from a parent? Imagine what it would have been like to have warm, loving, supportive parents who made time to speak with you every day about your tumultuous adolescent life. Just a hug and a smile when we got home from school would have reassured us enough to lighten up our own grim analysis of the day.

When the notion that we aren't loved or valued follows us into adulthood, we relate to others through maladaptive coping skills rather than our confident, authentic selves. This is a lonely place to live. Truly satisfying connections cannot be developed from this state of being.

> "You may have a general sense that you're missing something that everybody else has, or that you're on the outside looking in. Something just isn't right, but it's hard to name. It makes you feel somehow set apart, disconnected, as if you're not enjoying life as you should."
>
> —Jonice Webb, *Running on Empty: Overcome Your Childhood Emotional Neglect*

If you experienced emotional neglect in your childhood, this results in confusing emotions and perceptions of yourself and the world that can persist for decades. As an adult woman, you may feel different from others or unable to trust yourself or others. Disconnection from yourself and others leads to pervasive loneliness.

The following is a holistic healing process I use personally and with my adolescent and adult clients to heal feelings of disconnection and loneliness. This meditation connects you with the love you carry in your own heart. When you feel lonely, it means you are disconnected from yourself. You truly have all the love you need right inside yourself.

Heart Connection Meditation

- Sit or lay down in a comfortable and quiet space.

- Put both hands, one on top of the other, over your breastbone (the middle of your chest).

- Take a few deep breaths—in through your nose and out through your mouth.

- Relax into your body and direct your attention to the sensations in your chest.

- Feel the sensations and emotions that come up. Whatever you sense or feel is just right for you (and you may be tearful).

- Stay like this for a few minutes and just notice, without analyzing or judging.

- Explore your unique experience with this. Ask yourself questions like, "What am I feeling? What am I noticing?"

- Keep breathing and noticing for a minimum of five minutes and slowly build up your time as you practice this.

- When you feel complete, take a moment to journal about your experience.

You may find that you started with one emotion, such as irritation, and then found a different emotion underneath, like sadness. Feeling into and writing about the sadness connects you to your true emotion and helps you process it. This type of authentic connection with yourself will alleviate the loneliness. You are becoming your own best friend.

— Part 2 —

Coping: Effects of Childhood Wounding in Adulthood

~

CHAPTER 5

Trouble Breaking Away

Most of my child clients have a long history of high sensitivity, irritability, and general difficulties with everyday life and relationships. When they reach their late teens and are expected to be more mature, handle more stress, and make decisions, they become overwhelmed. This is when they typically seek help for what has developed into an anxiety disorder and/or depression. They continue growing but not maturing, staying stuck in maladaptive coping skills. Avoiding or clinging to their peers rather than participating in mature relationships causes them to feel separate from others. Not truly knowing or understanding themselves creates chronic discontent. Their habits of anticipating every problem and fearing any type of failure contribute to patterns of indecisiveness.

Adolescence and young adulthood are the natural times for kids to figure out who they are as individuals apart from their family. They have a strong desire to break out of their roles, take off the masks, and find their true selves. This takes great fortitude, and in that pursuit, their learned coping skills start to feel constricting. But if you experienced an emotionally neglectful childhood, that fortitude will likely be missing, causing you to either comply or fight with your parents. Family dysfunctions already in place may escalate as the teen naturally tries to pull away.

As you tried to break away from your family, do you remember trying to express a different opinion, pleading your case for more freedom, or setting your own priorities? How did that go? The following stories may help you understand why that time in your life was so difficult. And why, as an adult woman, you may still feel discontent, indecisive, and separate from others.

Discontent

I met Megan when she was sixteen and suffering from anxiety. It had been with her for many years and worsened in high school. Growing up, Megan experienced an emotionally volatile relationship with her mother and emotionally neglectful relationships with her father and stepfather. There was no safe harbor—no adult in her life who provided emotional support. Also, Megan was cast in the adult role of caretaker. She saw herself as her younger sister's protector while no one was taking care of her. She avoided social interactions, suffered from panic attacks and dissociation, and had no close friends.

Now twenty, Megan is still unhappy about how her life is going. She feels overwhelmed with managing relationships with her parents, dissatisfied with her college experience, bored with her job, and guilty because she has no motivation or interest in anything. Megan is stuck. She did have a romantic relationship, but it only stirred up insecurities about being lovable. Megan is very insightful and aware that something is wrong with how she relates and how little she feels for people. Jonice Webb puts it this way in her book, *Running on Empty*:

> When a child's emotions are not acknowledged or validated by her parents, she can grow up to be unable to do so for herself. As an adult, she may have little tolerance for intense feelings or for any feelings at all. She might bury them, and tend to blame herself for being angry, sad, nervous, frustrated, or even happy. The natural human experience of simply having feelings becomes a source of secret shame. "What is wrong with me?" is a question she may often ask herself.

Megan faithfully shows up for her appointments and truly wants to get unstuck and to feel more. We are working on how she can allow her feelings to surface, accept and understand herself better, and then create a life she can enjoy.

Separate

When I started to think about pursuing a bachelor's degree in nursing, I was in a secretarial program at the local community college. This was the only acceptable choice for me according to my parents. It was inexpensive and close enough to home that I had no reason to move out. I felt very restricted and left behind as I watched my peers experience the excitement of going away to college. I was still very much alone with no one to bounce ideas around with or help me make a plan for continuing my college education. I remember mailing the college application in the post office and thinking I was taking a leap of faith, knowing nothing about college life or how I would pay for it. But I just knew it was part of the bigger life I imagined for myself that included a professional career.

After graduating from community college with a degree in secretarial studies, I went directly to the local state college to major in nursing and was finally able to move out of the house. My mother was in treatment for breast cancer at that time, and I thought, "Now it's my father's turn to take care of her." I pretended to care, though. I went home every weekend out of habit or guilt to do laundry and avoid the fact that I had no social life.

Still, I remember walking around the college campus feeling thrilled and honored to be there. I could feel my potential with all this knowledge available. I was happy and hopeful for the first time in my life. I did nothing but work, go to classes, and do homework. I had no close friends, a few superficial friends, and no boyfriends. You could count on one hand the number of dates I had over the entire five years of my college experience. Most of the time, I was alone. And yet I felt I was better than my peers—more serious about my studies, not a partier. This mindset was a defense mechanism to cover my underlying and pervasive social anxiety that kept me separate from those around me.

During this time, out of both necessity and avoidance, I worked every weekend and holiday in the local hospital emergency room as a receptionist. I lived with a half-dozen other girls in a run-down duplex apartment, paying my own bills. All my time was spent going to classes, working, or studying. I did go out dancing with my roommates about three times a year. It was fun, but I was very anxious around young men. I felt no emotional connection with anyone. I understand now that I had internalized the belief that emotional connection meant having to take on the responsibility for someone else's problems. It was more comfortable to keep myself separate, even though I desperately longed for close relationships.

Indecisive

My client Jenny is a highly sensitive, empathic, and caring young woman. She has just graduated from college and is living with her parents. Even though she had made great progress in counseling over the past few years, her home environment is still quite challenging. Jenny had been working to alleviate her severe anxiety, panic attacks, agoraphobia, and low self-esteem without using medication. But after moving back with her parents, she decided that medication was necessary. She could tolerate the arguing, stonewalling, criticism, and general discontent that pervaded her home life, but it depleted her energy, leaving her with no resources to continue to heal.

Jenny has a full-time job in a doctor's office, but she really wants to go to medical school. We've discussed what a great doctor she would be, and she has come to believe this about herself. However, passing the entrance exam and applying to medical school feels daunting. She can't decide if it's worth spending money on the exam and spending time to study. Fears of failing, not getting accepted to medical school, and being unable to pay off loans keep her paralyzed. Jenny's habit of catastrophizing causes anticipatory anxiety and locks her in a state of indecision.

A Holistic Healing Process

When we grow up in an emotionally chaotic family, we learn to be on the lookout for the next shoe to drop, the next fight, the next critical remark. This habit of vigilance and anticipating every possible scenario takes all of our energy. We then tend to apply this maladaptive coping skill to every situation in our life. It was impossible for Jenny to develop clear decision-making skills while in constant reaction to her environment. Now, as a young adult, she is held back from her dreams because she focuses on all that could go wrong and is unable to commit to a decision.

Do you relate to these stories? What is *your* story about breaking away from your family? Sometime during your teens or young adulthood, you may have started to realize that something wasn't right; maybe you were being used, treated badly, or just ignored. As you tried to break away, you may have looked to your peers for meaningful relationships but they never filled the void and you experienced chronic discontent. Or you were unskilled at socializing and felt separate from others, always going it alone.

Did you have trouble deciding how to transition to adulthood? College sounded possible, but what major? Getting a job made sense, but where? You could take a gap year, but how? Maybe you took off and traveled just to get out of your house and away from your family. Whatever you did, it was likely in reaction to a problematic home environment which gave you only two options: going along with your parents' plans for you or breaking away without their support. You were either held back or catapulted forward by an emotional reaction which impaired your decision-making skills.

As an adult woman, poor relationship and decision-making skills may still be haunting you. Have you left a lot of people behind by not following through with keeping in touch? Do you secretly complain that you contact your friends more than they contact you? You may often feel lonely or rejected and wonder why. Your friendships and romantic relationships don't feel meaningful or fulfilling. You may wonder sometimes how you got to where you are today, feeling dissatisfied with your job or your living situation. Did you truly make conscious decisions to create your life or are you on autopilot? This can be hard to admit. We naturally want to defend the life we've built.

The following holistic healing process will help you understand yourself better so you can make decisions based on your own wants and needs. As a result, you will start to experience contentment with your life and more meaningful connections with your friends and family.

A Meditation to Connect with Your Higher Self

With this meditation, you will connect with and receive your own personal wisdom. Your "higher self" is the non-physical part of you that holds all the information you need for this lifetime. Your higher self will only give you information you are ready to hear. You may call it your soul or spirit or something else—whatever has meaning for you. This is not about praying, begging, or pleading. Use a confident tone and expect to get what you need.

- **Sit** or lay down in a quiet space. Close your eyes. Have your journal nearby.

- **Begin** to breathe slowly and deeply for a few minutes to settle your body.

- **Say** out loud, "Higher self, I need help."

- **Start** to whisper or just ponder in your mind these questions:

  - **What** are my talents and abilities?
  - **What** are my longings and dreams?
  - **What** is in my highest good?
  - **What** is my highest potential?

- **With** each question, wait quietly for answers to come to you. Your mind may want to chime in with thoughts and ideas. Just let them pass by for now.

- **Wait** and listen.

- **Answers** may come that cause emotions to surface. Do not analyze or doubt them. Just feel them. This is a sign you are on the right track.

- **Continue** this way for a few minutes or as long as you are comfortable.

- **When** you feel that you are finished, open your eyes and journal what you learned and felt.

~

CHAPTER 6

Limitations at Work

As adult women who experienced childhood emotional neglect, we carry childlike thinking that limits our career opportunities. Long-held, distorted beliefs about ourselves, others, and the world affect our perceptions of our abilities and the choices we make. Negative coping behaviors learned in childhood such as hiding, deferring to others, or lying inhibit our communication skills and ability to cooperate in our work environment. If you were frequently criticized or expected to be perfect, you may react with high anxiety when something goes wrong at work, judging yourself as incompetent. This leads to applying self-criticism to motivate yourself to do better: "What's the matter with me?" or "How could I mess up again?" It isn't normal to be constantly evaluating yourself and always "coming up short." It's unkind, unfair, and damages your self-worth. This is a learned, fear-driven behavior that can be unlearned for a happier, more satisfying work experience.

Avoiding conflict, brushing off poor treatment, blaming others for your feelings, or putting yourself down are common behaviors of people who experienced childhood emotional neglect. Are you always wondering if you are doing your job well enough? When you make a mistake, do you escalate into feeling completely incapable? Do you downplay your achievements or go above and beyond what is expected but still don't feel safe in your job? Maybe you feel like you work harder than anyone else, but you're not appreciated. You may secretly know you could do your boss's job, but anxiety and low self-worth keep you from going for it. Experiencing these difficult feelings regularly limits our performance and enjoyment at work. You may recognize these beliefs and behaviors in yourself as you read the following stories.

Unappreciated

Keri works as a laboratory technician in a hospital. She has been my coaching client for one year to help manage her anxiety, chronic high stress levels, and several physical health issues. Her demeanor and facial expressions show that she is at the edge of breaking down most of the time. Keri's life *is* overwhelming with three children, a full-time job, and a husband who works more than she does. She finds herself yelling at her children, experiencing panic attacks at work, and feeling chronically angry with her husband. At each session, Keri talks about how exhausted she is but shoots down every idea we discuss. I've suggested strategies such as, "How can you carve out some time for yourself to recharge?" or "Can you talk to your boss about decreasing your hours?" She is unwilling to ask for medical leave or even just an exemption from over-time. Communicating her level of dysfunction to her boss is unimaginable.

Keri doesn't advocate for the care and apprecia-tion she deserves because she fears confrontation. Due to an emotionally neglectful and chaotic childhood, she has no experience with stating her needs and peace-fully negotiating a solution. Her anxious mind tells her she must comply with what is expected and that her personal needs are inconsequential. She considers revealing her problems as complaining, which would cause shame and guilt that she can't tolerate. This painful, distorted thinking leads to blaming others with thoughts like, "Work is unfair" and "My boss doesn't like me."

So, Keri stays in the illusion that the job is the problem and it's other people's fault that she feels trapped with no solutions. She wants her boss to see that she is suffering and offer a solution without her having to say anything. This is childlike thinking—hoping others will solve her problems like a parent would for a child. She is looking for the parent/child relationship she didn't experience in childhood.

Because the situation is unlikely to play out this way, Keri will feel less and less appreciated, which will likely increase her irritability, anger, and resentment. She is at risk for generating more chronic illnesses, making mistakes at work which may lead to getting fired, and making an emotionally driven decision to quit, possibly sabotaging her career and reputation.

Unworthy

I saw my client, Elise, for about five months. She is a young woman in her mid-twenties who is trying to work her way up in a financial career. Elise suffered with anxiety, which causes her to feel chronically irritated and to sometimes lash out at people. Growing up in an emotionally volatile home full of stonewalling, yelling, and criticism, she had to fight for what she wanted. She never felt secure that she would get what she needed, and she has carried this lack of trust into her workplace. This has caused her to feel jealous and resentful of others in higher positions. During our time together, she was willing to learn communication techniques to help her get the promotion she wanted, but she was unable to see that she must also take responsibility for managing her emotional reactions at work. When she didn't get the promotion, she felt cheated and then discontinued her coaching sessions.

Deep below all of her emotions and behaviors is a feeling of unworthiness that Elise was unable to discuss. The message she received in her childhood home was that she wasn't worthy of fair and kind treatment. As an adult, this distorted belief affects the way she perceives herself and the world. When she returned to coaching one year later, Elise was managing her anxiety and communicating a little better, but she still carried anger and resentment as she saw others being promoted ahead of her. I encouraged her to become more aware of her thoughts and to check them with reality in the moment they came up so she could more effectively and directly communicate her needs instead of reacting out of insecurity. Unfortunately, Elise was still fighting for her self-worth. Brené Brown said it best in her book, *Daring Greatly*: "You either walk inside your story and own it, or you stand outside your story and hustle for your worthiness."

Incapable

When I graduated with my bachelor's degree in nursing, I was excited to start my first job as an RN. I chose a large hospital where there would be lots of opportunities to experience different kinds of positions. My knowledge and love of the work allowed me to start out feeling confident. Over time, however, my emotionally neglectful childhood caused me to become anxious, insecure, overly accommodating, and easily intimidated. I was constantly nervous about getting something wrong and the work became unsatisfying. This affected my ability to communicate effectively (an important part of the job), and my confidence soon eroded. I felt incapable, even though I knew I was good at my job.

There was a particular episode when a doctor yelled at me over the phone. I had called him late at night to tell him his surgical patient wasn't able to urinate. I proposed putting in a catheter to help her and then removing it to prevent infection. He told me to put in a permanent catheter. I started to make a case for my solution when he interrupted me. In an angry voice, he told me to do it his way, and then hung up. This was the best solution for *his* convenience, not for the patient. I was disillusioned and disappointed. I had expected respectful collaboration on patient cases, but hospitals are hierarchical. I became unable to communicate under stress. Any type of conflict, yelling, meanness, or disrespect put my nervous system into overload. Sparked by my call with that doctor, I decided I could no longer tolerate that work environment.

I switched to the pediatric unit where things were quieter and less intense. Everyone was nicer and I worked with mostly women. There were fewer emergencies, children were better behaved, and they recovered more quickly. I realized I had more empathy for sick children than for sick adults. I let go of my plan to try different nursing positions and committed myself to pediatrics. My inability to communicate professionally under stress had limited my career choices. I'll never know what more I could have learned or accomplished because I let my fears and not my natural talents direct my career. Fortunately, I landed in a specialty I truly enjoyed, which led me to become a pediatric nurse practitioner.

You might remember from an earlier childhood story that conflict avoidance has been a problem my entire life. For many years into my adulthood, I was unable to tolerate conflict. Someone else's anger meant I was inadequate and disappointing. I couldn't separate my worth from their emotional reactions and judgments. An angry, mean tone was enough to launch me into fear and self-blame while I frantically looked for ways to accommodate the other person.

A Holistic Healing Process

When your true self is unknown to you or hidden beneath your coping mechanisms because of childhood emotional neglect, you are prevented from accessing your natural talents and abilities. As an adult woman, you may struggle with work satisfaction because you don't know what kind of work fits your natural talents. Therefore, you may constantly experience self-doubt at work. And you may have already realized that changing to a new job doesn't solve the problem. The answer lies in building your self-worth and self-knowledge. It is also important to dedicate time every day for practicing self-care strategies. These are the key to keeping your nervous system balanced, quieting negative thoughts, and changing your beliefs and behaviors. I can teach and inspire my clients during a session, but they have to prioritize and practice new thoughts and behaviors in their daily lives. Reading inspirational poetry, like "A Morning Offering" by John O'Donohue, can help you make and keep the commitment of doing, saying, and believing something new that supports the life you want.

The following healing process will help you to change your thoughts and judgments about yourself and discover your capabilities and strengths. It will also help you change your focus from what went wrong to what went well.

Past Successes Journaling

1. Sit in a quiet place with your journal, take a few deep breaths.

2. Allow your mind to relax.

3. Begin to recall any positive experiences from your past work environments.

4. Negative experiences may come to mind first, let them pass through without reacting.

5. Practice redirecting and refocusing your thoughts by asking yourself the following questions:

   a. What went well?
   b. What parts did I enjoy?
   c. What capabilities do I possess that made things go well and feel enjoyable?

6. Write down anything that comes up even if you don't believe it's significant.

For example, when I asked a current coaching client these questions, she recalled an outing she had organized for the children she worked with. She kept saying it was no big deal because she didn't get recognition or payment for her efforts. The event was a success; she and the kids really enjoyed it. As I encouraged her to list what it took to make this happen, she was able to see her skills of organization, inspiration, communication, and dedication and own them as unique capabilities and strengths. This new insight helped her believe in herself and guided her search for a new job. She called this process "inside-out coaching"!

~

CHAPTER 7

Roles and Relating

Childhood emotional neglect distorts our perception of what a loving relationship feels like. Most likely, you were missing caring behaviors in your early childhood, like hugs, smiles, compliments, listening, or genuine interest in your ideas. "Attachment security happens in the first three years of life," writes Gabor Maté and Gordon Neufeld in *Hold On to Your Kids*. You may not have witnessed or participated in relationships that held warmth or tender moments where love could be felt. Perhaps you didn't feel emotionally safe asking for comfort, or you felt anxious not knowing when sweetness would turn into anger. Maybe you took on a specific role like "good girl" or "caretaker" to gain positive attention. You may have felt uneasy, sensing that something was missing but unable to identify it because you didn't have the experience of a loving relationship with attentive parents. These are the hidden injuries of childhood emotional neglect.

When the parent doesn't model loving behaviors and emotions, the child won't learn how to express them in future relationships. As an adult woman, relationships may then feel like a fight to win the other person's love, attention, or approval, causing anxiety and insecurity. It can make us feel too vulnerable to show our true self—our perceived neediness, weirdness, and messy emotions. Due to childhood wounding, our genuine true self was undeveloped in our early years and never became available to our conscious mind. Instead, we developed a finely tuned persona that sought to fit other people's needs, a persona we have carried into our adult relationships. We use our childhood coping skills of reading emotions, anticipating needs, and people pleasing to assess a situation and then react, speak, and/or behave in ways that are appealing or "won't cause trouble."

As a result, we can become a walking defense system with an armored heart, always scanning for trouble, unable to truly relax and genuinely connect with another person. In so doing, we miss out on the fullness of our own humanity. Going through life in this highly perceptive but preprogrammed, almost robot-like way feels empty and unfulfilling.

And so, we are drawn to fairy tales with happy endings and/or prescribed societal roles such as heterosexual girlfriend, partner, or wife. If we play the role just right—being quiet and nice, accommodating, and pretty—we might get the love we crave. Adopting cultural beliefs and expectations and copying superficial behaviors provide a framework for what relationships are supposed to look like. So, we follow a seemingly sure path to partnership where we think we will be happy at last, all our insecurities solved, with someone to love us forever. This is often how adult women with emotional wounds participate in romantic relationships because they don't possess the necessary skills for true connection.

But there is no escaping the past if you haven't done any personal growth work. You will inevitably bring your childhood wounds and childlike beliefs and behaviors into the partnership. You might feel like you love your partner, but how often do you also feel you are "going through the motions" or walking on eggshells? How often do you feel ignored as you imagine what they are feeling or thinking? Are you avoiding rejection by not speaking up for yourself or asking for what you want? The appearance of normalcy that is empty of meaning and depth is a stressful way to live.

The following stories are examples of how our own distorted thinking, beliefs, and behaviors are damaging our relationships more than we know. Notice if you recognize yourself in Susan's story of feeling ignored, my story of feeling rejected, or Judy's story of feeling empty.

Ignored

Susan is a professional woman in her forties. She is disillusioned with her fifteen-year relationship with her partner, the father of her daughter. She has been my coaching client for several months with the goal of leaving her partner. During this time, Susan has come to see how much she has compromised her ideals. Her partner has his own goals and plans, which Susan thought were compatible with her ideas of what she wanted in life. As she examined her relationship more closely, she realized how little respect and appreciation she receives in this relationship. During the first few weeks of coaching, Susan continued to blame her partner, exploding in anger while obviously burdened with a load of disappointment. She felt her partner had completely ignored her needs and wants. She believed that fighting, stonewalling, demanding, and threatening were her only options to be seen and heard.

Susan grew up in a household with parents who used fighting to solve problems—although nothing was ever solved. The house was filled with a tension that left her feeling anxious and restless to move out. Her mother was so preoccupied with her own anger that she was not aware of how it affected Susan or the behavior she was modeling for her daughter. This is where Susan learned to fight for attention, but even then, her needs were rarely considered.

As an adult, Susan was still using all of her energy to rail against being ignored while putting little effort into filling her own needs. All of her thoughts and actions were a reaction to her partner's behavior—not directed to her own benefit. As Susan started to understand the childhood source of these beliefs and behaviors, she became more motivated to make personal changes and model healthy communication for her daughter. She realized that she had been giving away her power—her agency over her life—to her partner. As these insights came up in our sessions, Susan would crinkle up her lip and squint her eyes. "Oh, my god, you're right!" She began to see her own self-worth: how hard she works, how well she cares for her daughter, and how resourceful she was in putting herself through college. Making the transition to being a single mom seems more attainable for Susan now that she has stopped ignoring herself.

Rejected

I was not myself during the two years before my divorce. I was consumed by anxiety and pulled under by depression. Though I covered it well most of the time, I was afraid of what my family would think of me in such a weakened state. The anxiety was related to starting and building my counseling practice at the age of fifty. At the same time, I was engaged in a personal development program and struggling to grow my self-worth and self-trust. But I blamed all my discontent on an unfulfilling marriage. I was in emotional pain and conflict and thought that if my partner changed, I could feel better. I wanted him to nurture me, reassure me, and show that he loved me in the ways I needed. But I didn't express this clearly to him. I just thought he should *know*. The few times I was able to speak up, I was vague and ashamed to share how I truly felt. I negatively interpreted everything he said and did.

In reality, it had less to do with him and more to do with me. I was judging, sabotaging, and, rejecting *myself*. In my tumultuous emotional state, I felt unworthy of love, so I couldn't see it or feel it when it was right in front of me. I was caught up in obsessive thoughts like, "He doesn't want to be with me. He doesn't really know me or value me." I never checked with him to see if any of this was true. Because my natural self-expression and self-advocacy were stifled in my childhood, I developed a habit of making up conversations in my mind. In my marriage, I got confused, thinking that I intuitively knew how he felt without actually asking him directly. And so, I created my own story in which he had rejected me but was too kind to say it.

The truth was, I didn't know or value myself. I was looking for the type of validation and love that a parent would give a child. I didn't want to take responsibility for my feelings; I just wanted to be comforted and reassured. Since I didn't receive this kind of love from my parents, I hadn't developed the capacity for mature love. And whenever my relationships felt distant or uncaring, it triggered feelings of loneliness and being unloved—*and* unlovable. I would then retreat, stay quiet, and go into hiding where nothing gets resolved. Feeling unworthy and unable to express myself or ask for what I needed became a trap that prevented me from checking my thoughts with the reality of the situation. Options for communication, compromise, or resolution were blocked. I was stuck in spiral thinking with no way out.

And so, instead of exploring ways to save the marriage, I believed the story in my head. I moved quickly through the divorce, thinking it would solve all my problems. My distorted perceptions convinced me that there was someone else out there who would be better for me, who would understand me and value me and express it in a way I could feel it. I still wasn't taking responsibility for my personal growth. I was looking for someone else to give me the love, appreciation, and compassion I didn't have for myself.

I continued with my personal development classes and even began to teach the program. Over the next three years, I learned about neuropsychology, communication in relationships, and childhood emotional neglect. I finally realized what happened to me: how and where my thinking became distorted and why I behaved the way I did. I knew that to move forward after the divorce, I had to practice self-compassion and forgive myself. I had to let go of judging my behavior during that time. If I had known myself and my history better, I would have managed the process differently. Maya Angelou said, "I did then what I knew how to do. Now that I know better, I do better." I've since learned how to forgive myself and let go of shame. I did the best I could with the knowledge and ability I had at the time. And I'm thankful for the new perspective and awareness.

With therapy and my own research and learning, I began to see myself and the situation more clearly. Feeling my own value for the first time, I stopped rejecting myself. I could see my sensitivity, intuition, and empathy as gifts, not weaknesses. I started focusing inward on my unique talents and abilities rather than outward to be validated by others. Clear-headed and on purpose, I felt better than I ever thought was possible. One of my favorite poems by Mary Oliver, "The Journey," kept me going.

Empty

When Judy started to entertain the idea that her decades-old marriage was over, she had been my coaching client for two years. She has known her husband since they were teenagers, and now they are in their fifties. Their only child had left home and Judy was feeling adrift, her life empty of meaning. As she turned her full attention to her husband, she realized they had not been true partners for a long time. She had been dutifully caring for his emotional needs while receiving no such support from him. Their marriage was running on shared despondency. They were so enmeshed in each other's lives, it was hard for Judy to see herself separate from him. His feelings were her feelings. She wondered what meaning she would find in a life without him. But over the years, the marriage had dissipated; there was no intimacy, no meaningful conversations, and no common ideals or shared dreams. They were going through the motions, their interactions becoming more and more superficial. She felt empty, sad, and stuck but unable to act for fear of hurting him.

Judy grew up with a demanding mother; you didn't want to cross her. From this harsh home environment, Judy learned to anticipate her mother's moods, lay low, and stay out of the way. Because there was no concern for Judy's emotional well-being, she internalized the belief that she wasn't worthy of care and attention. She never learned that she deserved to be considered and have her emotional needs met. This caused her to believe that other people's needs come first in a relationship. As a married adult woman, she put her husband's emotional needs before her own for twenty-five years, which left her feeling exhausted and empty.

Over the next four years, I saw Judy on and off as she slowly turned her focus to her own personal growth. As she grew in self-knowledge and self-worth, she grew apart from her husband, who stayed in his negative mindset and chronic depression. It took that much time for Judy to extricate herself from her marital enmeshment and allow her husband to take responsibility for improving his life. She quit using all of her energy to be her husband's life raft. With more compassion for herself, an elevated mood, and increased energy, she started filling her emptiness with the people and experiences that *she* desired. Judy came to believe that her happiness was her responsibility and that she deserved a full, equal partnership in this new vibrant life she dreamed of.

A Holistic Healing Process

When I speak to women about changing their self-expression to honor their true self, all they can think of is how their partner will react. This reflects our fear of being unlovable, developed in a childhood that conveyed the message that love is conditional. We innately fear being kicked out of the tribe we naturally crave belonging to, so it can feel very risky to let go of habitual communication patterns.

Here are some of the ways we avoid direct, honest communication:

- Suppressing strong feelings, anything from anger to love.
- Hesitating to show spontaneous affection.
- Difficulty giving and receiving compliments.
- Using sarcasm or jokes to convey feelings.
- Being silent or just using a facial expression.
- Complaining without offering a solution.
- Apologizing too much.

We tell ourselves all kinds of stories to justify this behavior: They won't listen anyway. We need to keep the peace. Better to be kind and giving. Be a good person. Don't be selfish. The truth is that you learned these ways of interacting and rationalizing as coping mechanisms in your childhood relationship with your parents—a role reinforced by the majority of societal messages for how to act as an adult woman. But below these confining stereotypes we often find emptiness and resentment reflected in such thoughts as, "Why am I the one who has to sacrifice all the time?" "How come they don't understand me?"

You now have the opportunity to decide if this type of identity and self-expression reflects your true self. You can take baby steps toward trusting your own voice, truth, and inner knowledge. When you disregard your needs and suppress your unique personality, the real you disappears. Real love only works when you are willing to be vulnerable and express your authentic self. The following is a Holistic Healing Process you can use to practice direct, clear communication in your relationships.

Self-Expression Practice

This practice will help you become more aware of your true feelings in the present moment and to express those feelings. You will learn to manage any emotions that come up and follow through on your intentions. Consider discussing this practice with your partner and ask for patience and support.

Follow these steps during an interaction with your partner:

1. Start with breathing and grounding. Ask yourself, "What am I really feeling right now?"

2. Use "I" statements. Talk about yourself only—your needs and your feelings.

3. Be direct and use concrete examples: Instead of, "How come you get to walk away and leave me with this mess?!", say "I'm overwhelmed with making and cleaning up after dinner. I need you to clear the table and load the dishwasher."

4. Choose your words carefully. Speak slowly and deliberately. Monitor your tone.

5. Listen to yourself. Are you escalating your emotions, complaining, or explaining too much? Or are you making a statement or request with confidence?

6. Count every time you speak up and express yourself as a win, even when your partner's reaction is not ideal. You didn't do it wrong because they reacted badly.

7. Keep your focus on yourself and your goals. This exercise is for your practice.

Do these activities on your own:

1. Practice singing, reciting poetry, or anything else that uses your voice. Get comfortable with hearing your voice.

2. Yell, cry, and/or talk out loud when you are alone. Practice a confident tone.

3. Notice what you feel about your voice. What messages and judgments are coming up from your childhood?

"And the day came when the risk to remain tight in a bud was more painful than the risk it took to blossom."

—Anais Nin

— Part 3 —

Healing: Holistic Healing Plan for Emotional Wounds

~

CHAPTER 8

Discovering Yourself

In order to heal all aspects of the self—body, mind, emotions, and spirit—it is necessary to use a holistic approach. You cannot simply focus on one area while ignoring the others. They are interdependent. For example, you may have experienced this when you started an exercise program but didn't meet your goals because you were undisciplined or sabotaged yourself with negative thinking. Maybe you sought spiritual growth but felt blocked because your emotions were overwhelming.

To begin to uncover your true self, you will need to dedicate a portion of your energy and time to your healing. Sometimes we only do this when life falls apart and we are forced to re-evaluate everything, such as during a divorce, a job loss, health issues, financial problems, or the death of a loved one. This is true for many of my coaching clients, some of whom come to me too late. All the parts of their lives they were juggling have come crashing down. They struggle with feeling lost, unfocused, exhausted, or all three. Some are suffering with anxiety, depression, or chronic anger. The good news is, you don't have to wait until it gets that bad. You can commit to your healing journey right now! And if you pay close attention, you will notice that a part of you knows this is necessary, that this work will be the bridge to building a life that reflects your true self.

The holistic healing work described in this final section has been formulated into a step-by-step plan that I developed over many years. During my own healing journey, I researched and tried many different practices including breath work, meditation, yoga, and journaling, and then gradually brought these practices to my clients. I noticed there was an order to the steps that worked best. No matter the diagnosis, my clients needed first to balance their nervous system to increase their energy and ability to commit to the daily practices. You may have tried such strategies as journaling or meditation and found they didn't help or you couldn't stay with them. That's likely because your brain was not prepared for them; it was still in a high-stress mode with poor focus, scattered thoughts, and little clarity.

Rollin McCraty, PhD, director of research at the HeartMath Institute, says, "We want to achieve a state where the nervous system is regulated, more stable, flexible, and harmonious." The practices in this chapter focus on healing your nervous system, which will help you feel more stable, relaxed, and comfortable as you begin your Holistic Healing Plan and move through to more advanced practices. Try to do at least one each day; baby steps are the best way to get to where you want to go. And don't forget to pat yourself on the back for staying committed to your well-being!

Self-Care

Our brain is wired to seek safety, satisfaction, and connection, so it watches out for any threat to these desired states. When we frequently feel emotionally unsafe, disappointed, or disconnected in our childhood, we become overly cautious, on alert for hurtful things that may happen again. This protective factor can become harmful as our body holds the tension of this chronic uncertainty. We end up walking through the world armed and defended even if we don't notice it. Are your shoulders or jaw tight and sore? Do you grind your teeth or have headaches? Does your mind overthink and overanalyze? The first time I realized I had been holding chronic tension was when I attended childbirth education classes at the age of thirty. The teacher taught us how to intentionally relax our muscles and vocalize through the pain. I noticed how tight I held my jaw and how I held my tongue to the roof of my mouth to keep my mouth closed. A few years later, after my second child was born, I started taking yoga classes. It was then that I found all the other places in my body holding tension.

There is a feedback loop between the brain and heart. Through neural connections, the heart conveys our emotional state to our brain, affecting our thinking patterns. A good example is chronic stress and anxiety, which cause our heart rhythm to fall out of balance. That information is sent to the brain, triggering thoughts that correspond with that feeling. Distorted thinking patterns (think "fight or flight") then ramp up, sending us into reaction mode while cutting off access to intentional thoughts and actions.

"The quality of the signals that our heart sends upstairs to our brain have a profound effect on how our brain works." says McCraty of the HeartMath Institute. When the heart and brain are in coherence (balanced), we gain clarity, focus, and judgment. HeartMath defines coherence as "a state in which the heart, mind. and emotions are balanced and operating in sync and the immune, hormonal, and nervous systems function in energetic coordination." Under this condition, our body shifts into healing mode rather than stress mode. We can then focus on the reality of the moment and respond appropriately. To get there, we need strategies for noticing when stress, worry, and tension are being triggered by painful emotions that happened in our past and not by something happening in the present moment. Knowing this difference is a key to healing.

A holistic approach to health and healing starts by acknowledging that there exists in our body a highly sensitive communication system—especially the heart, which senses the entire body and feeds that information to the brain. When a healthy brain receives a signal that something is wrong in the body, it makes decisions and plans to correct it. When we ignore those signals, such as those reflecting chronic high stress, our emotions and thoughts fall into unhealthy patterns and our body suffers. This is why we get headaches, nausea, or experience poor sleep when stressed. Our body is expressing a dysfunction in the system. When we try to cheat this system, we become progressively debilitated, not just physically but mentally, emotionally, and spiritually. Prioritizing and caring for yourself must come first before any healing will take place. For example, what commitments can you reduce or let go of to focus more on *your* needs? How can you simplify your life and make room for self-care?

Below you will find stress-reducing practices including diaphragmatic breathing, self-awareness building, visualization. Practiced daily, these strategies will bring your heart into coherence, calm the nervous system, and begin to heal the effects of emotional wounding on the body, mind, and emotions. Self-care is your responsibility. Committing to daily self-care is an act of kindness, gentleness, and reverence for your true self.

Daily Breathing and Body Scan

To decrease stress, repair your nervous system, increase awareness of tension, and shift your body into healing mode

1. **Sit** or lie down in a quiet space, get comfortable, and close your eyes.

2. **Take** a moment to settle your mind and focus on your body.

3. **Notice** your breathing without trying to change it.

4. **Start** to breathe in through your nose and out through your mouth.

5. **Gently** deepen your breath down to the bottom of your lungs and then blow it all out.

6. **Repeat** slowly and evenly.

7. **If** your focus returns to your thoughts, gently bring it back to your body.

8. **Notice** any tension in your body by doing a body scan:

   - Relax your facial muscles, eyes, and jaw.
   - Soften your neck and shoulders.
   - Notice your chest going up and down with your breathing.
   - Relax your belly.
   - Allow your hips to get heavy.
   - Loosen your legs, arms, hands, and feet.

9. **Continue** breathing and scanning the body for 3–5 minutes.

10. **Open** your eyes and notice how you feel.

Even a simple daily breathing practice can break unhealthy thinking patterns and facilitate whole system healing. Biofeedback games from HeartMath Institute, for example, have helped my clients to see the effects of their breathing on heart coherence and encouraged them to keep practicing and improving their technique. Parents and their kids will practice together in my office and then daily at home. I am always amazed that most children feel the calming effects after one session. Parents also enjoy the exercise though the effects take longer.

Daily Awareness Process

To balance your emotions and bring them to conscious awareness

- **Allow** yourself time and space for underlying emotions and feelings to surface such as sadness, resentment, exhaustion, or feeling taken advantage of.

- **Acknowledge** these emotions and feelings as they come up without self-judgment or making up a story about them. They are all valid.

- **Accept** your current state of being, sit with the sensations, and claim them as your own to feel and heal. Avoid negative *or* positive labels and don't blame others.

- **Become** aware of where you feel the emotion in your body, such as a churning stomach, tension headache, or an aching heart.

Now notice what would feel good right now such as a glass of water, breathing, or even crying. Go ahead and take care of yourself and then write about your experience with this process and how it felt to respond to your own needs in the moment.

Grounding Visualization

To recharge your body, reclaim your energy, stop obsessive thinking, dissociation, distraction, and numbness, and facilitate focus, calm, attention, and clarity

- **Your** body is your home. The earth is your charging station.

- **Get** comfortable and still, take a few deep breaths, and close your eyes.

- **Feel** your feet on the floor and imagine energy coming up from the ground through your feet and into your body.

- **Imagine** pulling all of your energy in from the environment around you—the people, situations, and circumstances.

- **Now** bring your focus out of your thoughts and into your body.

- **Notice** your breathing as you continue to imagine stabilizing earth energy coming up through you and all your own energy coming back into you.

- **Feel** a sense of the clear, calm energy now available to you.

- **Open** your eyes when you feel relaxed and recharged.

Self-Knowledge

To avoid emotional pain in your childhood, you may have stopped expressing your authentic opinions, preferences, needs, wants, and desires. One way of recognizing this is when trying to answer the question, "What do you remember enjoying as a young child?" If you only have a few vague memories, most likely you missed out on a childhood unique to you. When you shaped your identity to fit your environment, you unconsciously suppressed your true self. So, who are you, really?

In his book, *Healing Collective Trauma*, Thomas Hübl asserts that we are swimming in the waters of trauma passed down through generations. We've normalized difficulty and, in commiserating about it, confirm that others are suffering as much as we are. We deal with life circumstances using our trusty coping skills while trying to make the best of things. We see ourselves as just getting by and definitely "not enough."

What would it be like if you could jump out of that mindset? What if it's possible to view yourself as not just capable, but amazing—a work of art, precious beyond belief? And that you are here to express your unique gifts for your own pleasure and the betterment of the world? To believe such things, you would have to be curious, present, and aware enough to question your habitual thinking and avoid automatic reactions. You would need to create a new reality with new thoughts and keep asking the question, "What am I focusing on?" You would take time to notice the thoughts that dominate your attention throughout the day. Because when we think differently, our perceptions will change and we will see our true self more clearly.

Because you experienced emotional wounding in childhood, many of your thoughts and beliefs are distorted by your childlike interpretation of current experiences and carry the charge of the emotions you felt at the time. Our thoughts run on neural pathways in the brain—one neuron connecting to the next one to create a thought and then a chain of thoughts. These chains become well-traveled trails. This is why you find yourself going down the same thought paths over and over again and having a hard time breaking the pattern. The neurons must physically break away from each other to create a new pathway for a new thought. This ability of the brain and its neural pathways to re-shape themselves is called *neuroplasticity*.

The brain responds to repetitive learning and practice. You can shift your unwanted thoughts, such as judgments of yourself and others, through daily attention. When a painful thought or belief comes into your conscious mind, allow the attached emotion to be felt in your body. As you tenderly repeat this process, you are clearing old programming out of your brain and body.

"The moment you change your perception is the moment you rewrite the chemistry in your body."

—Bruce Lipton, *The Biology of Belief*

The following practices are designed to help you develop new thoughts and beliefs that reflect your true self. You will rewire your brain to think and perceive in a way that is authentic and beneficial to you. You may have heard the adage, "Neurons that wire together, fire together." By thinking differently and creating new neural circuits, you will change habitual thought patterns that will positively affect your mood, energy, and behavior.

Assets List

To get in touch with your unique, complex self and understand yourself in a new way

1. **As** you go through your day, start noticing what you are good at and what you enjoy.

2. **Avoid** focusing on what you do for others or how you make them feel. Keep your focus on your own feelings and what you are experiencing in each moment.

3. **Every** evening, create a column on a page or in a journal and write down a few things you noticed from the day—no matter how small—that felt good, rewarding, or like your natural self. Maybe it was talking to a friend, finishing a work project, or eating delicious food.

4. **Then** make a second column and write down corresponding assets you possess that made those

experiences enjoyable. What is it in you that is able to appreciate those things? For example, if you really enjoyed your lunch, your asset may be Food Connoisseur!

5. **Continue** to watch for these experiences and journal them. Read over the entire list daily.

Past Successes Journaling

To change your thoughts and judgments about your capabilities and strengths

1. **Bring** to mind a recent experience that you have been judging yourself about, such as not speaking up in a conversation.

2. **Sit** in a quiet place with your journal and take a few deep breaths.

3. **Allow** your mind to relax.

4. **Begin** to recall positive experiences from your past related to the current problem, like a time you were assertive in a conversation.

5. **Negative** experiences may come to mind first; let them pass without reacting.

6. **Practice** redirecting and refocusing your thoughts to those positive experiences by asking yourself the following questions:

    - **What** went well?
    - **What** felt good?
    - **What** capabilities do I possess that made those things go well?

7. **Write** down anything that comes up even if you don't believe it's significant. For example, maybe you felt at ease with the people you were talking to or you felt brave because you shared something that was important to you or your confidence got people's attention. Writing about it helps you to start to believe and remember that you possess such capabilities and attributes.

Visualization for Self-Knowledge

To uncover your personal beliefs and values and try on a new version of yourself

1. **Sit** down, take a few breaths, and close your eyes.

2. **In** your mind, picture yourself alone in a field with the sun shining on you. You are free to do as you please. No one is watching you.

3. **You** have no roles to play and no rules to follow.

4. **What** are you feeling? What do you look like? What are you doing?

5. **Who** are you outside the roles of mother, wife, partner, girlfriend, daughter, friend, worker, or boss?

6. **Who** are you outside of the rules laid down by authorities like religion, culture, society, government, and family?

7. **Consider** these questions and stay in the visualization as long as you like.

8. **When** you are ready, open your eyes and journal your experience.

9. **Try** the following prompts to get started:

- **What** would you believe about yourself or change in your life if all your roles and rules fell away?
- **What** personal values arise from your true self when you drop all the expectations that come with these roles and rules?
- **How** would those values shape your choices, behaviors, and beliefs?
- **What** would be different in your life?

As you journal, notice any thoughts that come up about your worthiness: "This is selfish." "I don't deserve this." "I'm fooling myself." These are examples of well-worn patterns running along those old neural pathways in your brain. They are false beliefs, not based in the reality of who you truly are. In coaching, we call them *saboteurs*. They keep you in stasis because new ideas are scary for a brain that has been on high alert for so long.

Earlier in the chapter, I asked, "So who are you, really?" These practices will help you answer that question. You will come to know yourself better and gain more insight into your true self. What might that feel like for you? I remember how it was for me: It felt expansive and empowering, like I was in the driver's seat of my life! With growing confidence and assertiveness, I finally felt like I belonged in the world. Anything was possible with my belief in myself and willingness to follow through on my own ideas. I was free to craft my own unique life that came from knowing my true self. As you free yourself from attachments to old beliefs about yourself and the world, your true self will shine through. As you expand into your full self, you will feel a bigger presence in your body—more energy and vitality. From this new vantage point, you will be ready to decide what you want your life to look like next.

~

CHAPTER 9

Opening Your Heart

Remember when we talked about those automatic thoughts that run on well-worn neural pathways in your brain? The emotions attached to those thoughts are stored in your body. When painful experiences are relegated to the unconscious part of your mind, the attached feelings get locked away in your body. This is called *repression*. When one of those memories comes to your conscious mind, it brings up attached emotions that need to be processed through your body. The practice of opening your heart helps with acceptance and compassion for yourself as those painful feelings surface. No more suppressing, no more ignoring. As you breathe into your heart space and allow *all* your feelings to be present, you become witness to your own childhood emotional wounds.

Later in this chapter, you will learn healing practices to help with this. Over time, the emotional charge will be unlocked from your body, neutralized, and become part of your life force energy. That's the cool part: You will gain energy from this process! As you go deeper with this work, more stuck energy is released. You will feel unburdened, lighter, and freer than you ever thought possible. During the times you feel alone and tender during this process, remember that this is your human journey, no different from any other human who chooses to walk this path. You are not alone. You are discovering the depths of your love in the depths of your sorrow.

In the poem, "The Guest House," Rumi eloquently tells us how and why we want to allow and experience all of our emotions:

This being human is a guest house.
Every morning a new arrival.
A joy, a depression, a meanness,
some momentary awareness comes
as an unexpected visitor.
Welcome and entertain them all!
Even if they're a crowd of sorrows,
who violently sweep your house
empty of its furniture,
still, treat each guest honorably.
He may be clearing you out
for some new delight.
The dark thought, the shame, the malice,
meet them at the door laughing,
and invite them in.
Be grateful for whoever comes,
because each has been sent
as a guide from beyond.

When I first started focusing on opening my heart as part of my healing journey, I couldn't feel anything. It just felt like a rock sitting in the middle of my chest. Some of you may know this from Hinduism as a blocked heart chakra. It comes from the stifled expression of love. A psychic once told me that she sensed a twelve-mile-thick concrete wall around my heart. I felt cold and shaky and actually sick when I heard that, but it felt true. Still, I thought of myself as a loving person, and it was a mystery to me at the time as to how and why my heart had developed such a protective layer. After exploring this for some time, I realized that I gave love out of obligation and insecurity. I was unconsciously asking the question: How much love can I get back from this interaction? Without being aware of it, I was highly focused on getting love from others to fill me up but never feeling full. And so, I was stingy with love, only giving as much as I felt I was getting. My loving attitude and behavior were motivated by reward. I was playing the role of nice, helpful, and caring woman to feel accepted and appreciated and calling it love.

When you start to focus on feeling into your heart, you may find sorrow. If so, let it flow. After a while, you may find calmness or gratitude. Then you may feel the subtle sensations of your heart waking up. When this happened to me, it felt at first like a clunking sensation in my heart area—I had forgotten about the concrete wall experience. For a few months, I woke up most nights with this clunking feeling. It wasn't a panic attack or an irregular heartbeat, and I intuitively knew I didn't need to see a doctor. It was my concrete wall breaking down. I just breathed through it, telling myself it was a good thing and crying with gratitude. My heart was recalibrating to the vibration of love. After that, I could feel warmth in my chest and envision sending and receiving love from my heart. When you become brave enough to give more love without attachment, you will feel love in and around you all the time.

Self-Responsibility

Believing that this is your personal work and mission will help you take full responsibility for it. The definition of responsibility is "able to respond," meaning you are the only one who can respond to your needs and own your feelings. In *Healing Collective Trauma*, Thomas Hübl writes, "...trauma is transmitted from one generation to the next—until it finds space and presence and clarity; until it is owned so that it may be healed." Anything outside of you will not heal you; they can only point the way to this work. All the Reiki, yoga, meditation, or other well-intentioned practices won't work alone. Your vulnerability and willingness to feel into these powerful emotions and memories is required.

Taking 100% responsibility for your emotions will feel messy, scary, *and* liberating. You will have to practice owning your emotions instead of blaming others. Whatever you condemn in others reflects your feelings about yourself. We project painful feelings onto others to avoid a painful truth about ourselves. For example, if you get angry when you see unfair behavior, you are either unfair to yourself or others or both. Your conscious mind doesn't want to know this about yourself. When you evaluate your emotions with curiosity instead of judgment, however, you will bring these habits into the light to be transformed. Your responsibility is to accept whatever comes up and trust that your feelings are valid and worth exploring. In so doing, you are being respectful and true to yourself and others for the first time. Be proud that you are in integrity—practicing honesty and sincerity at all times. Hold yourself with unwavering compassion as you stumble through this experiment of opening your heart.

As you assume responsibility for your emotions, you will naturally become an expert at listening to your body. Opening your heart requires open communication with your entire body, which is longing for your love and attention. Remember: It's the vehicle through which you get to live your precious life. Contrary to what most women have been conditioned to believe, you can trust your body as your ally. Like your best friend, it's got your back and wants to serve you. There is no need to fear it, tame it, or treat it. Cherish your body. Listen and respond to it as if it's a beloved child. Your body holds the messages you need to hear on your unique healing journey.

Embodiment Practice

To practice listening to messages from your body. Your body is your ally in healing your emotions. Feeling into your body is the gateway to emotional freedom.

- Throughout the day and night, notice without judgment sensations from your body.

- Accept what comes up. You may experience stomach pains, difficulty breathing, a tight chest, tense muscles, a headache, or something else.

- Be present with each sensation and breathe through it.

- Acknowledge that it's there to draw your attention to stuck energy.

- Be kind and care for yourself in these moments.

- Thank your body for alerting you to imbalances.

- Find a gentle movement practice you enjoy that helps to improve your body awareness and become more present with your body feelings.

"Free Your Energy" Journaling

To unlock stuck energy in the body by naming emotions related to body sensations, honoring them with focused attention, then reinforcing the learning by journaling your experience

1. What emotions correspond with the physical sensations you experienced from your embodiment practice from above? For example, the sensation/feeling of nausea is related to the emotions of fear or anxiety. The feeling of a tight chest is related to the emotions of anger or sadness.

2. Where, when, or with whom have you felt these sensations?

3. Name a specific emotion to acknowledge, honor, and own it: "I have sadness in me."

4. Breathe as you focus on the emotion; notice if any energy shifts or release or if your heart begins to soften.

5. Reassure yourself that you are strong enough to do this practice. If you feel overwhelmed, you can stop anytime or choose to practice with shorter sessions.

6. Journal your experience:
   - Write down the true emotion underneath the feeling from your body.
   - Try to identify when and/or where the emotion originated in your life.
   - Note any changes in your energy.

The more you consciously process your emotions, the stronger and braver you will feel. You will gain more energy to keep going. This becomes a positive feedback loop where you start to trust the process and yourself. You learn to trust that all your emotions are valid and you have a right to feel them and process them for your personal growth. You'll be amazed at how your energy will soar!

Heart Connection Meditation

To reconnect with your heart energy, process hidden emotions, and facilitate emotional healing

1. **Sit** or lay down in a comfortable and quiet space.

2. **Put** one hand on top of the other over your breastbone (the middle of your chest).

3. **Take** a few deep breaths—in through your nose and out through your mouth.

4. **Relax** into your body and direct your attention to the sensations in your chest.

5. **Feel** the sensations and emotions that come up. Whatever you sense or feel is just right for you (and you may be tearful).

6. **Stay** like this for a few minutes and just notice, without analyzing or judging.

7. **Explore** your unique experience with this. Ask yourself questions like, "What am I feeling? What am I noticing?"

8. **Keep** breathing and noticing for a minimum of five minutes and slowly build up your time as you practice this.

9. **When** you feel complete, take a moment to journal about your experience.

You may find that you started with one emotion, such as irritation, and then found a different emotion underneath, like sadness. Feeling into and writing about the sadness connects you to your *true* emotion and helps you process it. This authentic connection with your heart will help you move through and out of despair, hate, envy, betrayal, and loneliness. Then the emotions of gratitude, appreciation, forgiveness, unconditional love, compassion, hope, tenderness, empathy, peace, and balance will have room to grow for your own healing.

Self-Expression

After working with the practices above for some time, you may notice an expansion of your heart's ability to feel as well as more clarity about what is true for you. You may acknowledge true feelings more often and find more compassion for yourself and others. As you begin to trust this experience, the next step is to actually express your true emotions to the people in your life. Inauthentic self-expression has been blocking you from meaningful, heart-centered relationships because you were not expressing from an open heart. Your expressions were colored by your habit of presenting a false self. Hiding your true feelings has been a way to avoid the insecurity of vulnerability. Your expressions have been unconsciously designed to protect you or manipulate the situation or other people into accepting, approving, or admiring you. Maybe your emotions feel too big or too complicated to express. Perhaps you believe that others won't understand or respond in a way that is helpful. You may be judging your intense emotions as too angry, too sentimental, too harsh, too pitiful, or too personal.

> "It may be helpful here to review my belief that within every negative feeling there is a longing, a wish, and, because of that, there is a recipe for success. It is the speaker's job to discover that recipe."
>
> —John Gottman, *The Science of Trust*

Due to childhood emotional wounding, you may never have honored your deep emotions or learned to express them. But our emotions come out one way or another. We all have a natural need to be heard, understood, cared for, and loved. To get these needs met, you may be expressing your emotions indirectly. Here are few examples of this:

- Manipulating to convince others without asking directly.

- Lying for fear of judgment or anger.

- Testing someone by being purposefully vague to see if they know your needs, which would prove he/she cares about you.

- Staying silent and using small signals of discontent while waiting for someone to ask you how you are.

- Acting sick or incapable to force someone into caring behavior.

With this way of communicating, there is never any satisfaction because your true self is not being seen or heard. Others are responding to the false self you are presenting rather than your true self, so the interaction is ultimately inauthentic.

Being a sensitive, empathic, and intuitive woman, you can get overwhelmed by the emotions you feel for loved ones and those around you—truly caring about people but unable to express it. You intuitively know that you have so much more to give, but past hurts from childhood keep you closed off.

I used to call all my family members every Saturday morning to connect with them. The exchange went something like this: How are you? Good. How are you? Good. So, what's been going on with you? And then they would tell me about their week, problems at work, with kids, general news. Even when they asked about my life, I would only say good or fine and maybe add some vague comments. I thought this was how to love people—being their sounding board. There were no meaningful exchanges with laughter or tears or encouragement or opinions. I truly didn't know how much real sharing was missing. These were superficial conversations so I could feel I did my duty and at least tried to connect. And yet my inner dialogue went like this: *They never call me or ask about my life. They don't care about me.* Do you see the disconnect? With such thoughts going around in my head, I didn't dare share highly personal feelings with them.

When you start to live your life with an open heart, you will experience the richness of true relationships—from the depths of sharing painful emotions to the heights of sharing excitement, admiration, and the sheer happiness of a moment. You will, however, have to reveal your true emotions, and it will feel risky and awkward, at least at first. But don't let that stop you. Practice expressing from your heart no matter the consequences—real or imagined. Dare to be vulnerable to criticism and misunderstanding. It's a given that some people won't understand or relate to you. If you feel disappointed when that happens, it's a clue that you are looking outside for validation. Instead, validate yourself by honoring your process and staying with it. Keep recommitting to your personal growth. It will feel wonderful when your self-expression feels natural and reflects your true self.

The following practices will help you to change how you express yourself so you can experience more meaningful and enjoyable interactions. You will become confident enough to express all that you feel in your heart without worry of judgment from others. An open heart enjoys giving and receiving love. An open heart is able to stay open while carefully applying boundaries as needed. An open heart is clear, truthful, authentic, and self-aware.

Saying "NO" – Setting Boundaries

To clearly and effectively express your "No" so you can be true to yourself and protect your time and energy.

Giving to others is something we naturally enjoy and want to do, but it's only rewarding when we have the energy to give. When we over-give, our energy becomes diluted and seeps into other people's lives like an amorphous blob without boundaries. Your time and energy belong to you, so when you put your own well-being first, you can participate in loving relationships while caring for yourself at the same time. To protect your energy, ask yourself the following questions:

- What is my energy level today?

- How does my body feel? Feel into your heart and gut.

- What is my body telling me? Trust the intuitive messages you receive and act on them. For example, if you truly have little energy and your body just wants a nap, honor that.

- What thoughts are coming up? Notice if they are coming from obligation or guilt.

- What is my willingness and/or interest level in giving what is being asked of me?

- Will I enjoy it? Is it important to me?

It's your responsibility to honor your boundaries by saying what is true for you in the moment. Here are some things to keep in mind as you practice authentic communication:

1. Be clear and precise, firm and kind, and don't over-explain.

2. Be conscious of how your expressions affect others; show compassion and empathy.

3. Allow others to react in their own way without trying to manage their emotions.

4. Manage your own emotions, expressions, and reactions.

5. Stay true to yourself in any compromise.

6. Decide if you want further interaction and then act on your decision.

Ways to say "No":

- That won't work for me.

- I'd rather do it this way.

- I need a break from talking about this.

- No thank you.

- I need to be alone.

- I'm not feeling well.

- I don't have time (only when this is true).

- That's not really my thing.

- Not now, maybe later.

True Self-Expression Practice

To get clear about how you feel in the moment and express yourself directly and truthfully.

The most effective strategy you can start to implement is to use "I" statements every time you talk about how you are feeling or what you need from others. This simple shift to using "I" instead of "you" will increase your self-awareness while helping you to own your emotions and be more accountable. As you do, watch out for the following:

- Saying, "You know when you feel...?" instead of "I feel..."

- Talking about the other person instead of yourself, like when you say, "You made me feel..." instead of "I feel..."

Some things to remember as you practice using "I" statements:

- You deserve to be heard and understood.

- It's your responsibility to be as clear as possible.

- Choose your words and tone carefully.

- You are being loving and kind to yourself and others.

- Be self-aware in the moment; notice how you are doing and correct yourself as needed.

Saying "YES" – Receiving

To elevate your self-worth so you can receive help, compliments, presents, or favors joyfully and gratefully.

If you have trouble accepting anything positive, it's because you don't feel worthy of it. You may have a belief that it's selfish or draws unwanted attention to you. You may have had childhood experiences that sent a message that you don't deserve nice things or compliments or that it's selfless to refuse offers of help. None of this is true. And so, as you practice saying yes more often, make note of the following:

- You will be affirming your true emotions and needs.

- When you say no to something you really want or need, you are not expressing your authentic self.

- Assume people are offering you something from their heart, not out of obligation

- Bonus: This practice of saying yes more often will open your eyes to the reality of how kind people are.

Here are some ways to say "Yes":

- Yes, I'd like that.

- Yes, thank you.

- Yes, that's nice of you.

- Yes, I appreciate that.

- Yes, please.

As you practice these healing strategies, it will get easier to know what you feel and how to express it. Opening your heart will allow you to feel everything more clearly and acutely. You may think this will feel overwhelming, but being responsible for your true feelings actually gives you more control. You are monitoring yourself for authenticity in each moment— re-examining your feelings and restating things as needed. As you continue to feel into your heart, you will start to honor and trust yourself more. You will know you are worthy of experiencing the whole range of human emotions. This will deepen your relationships and grow into an all-encompassing love in your heart. If you allow it, this can become your natural state of being throughout your life.

~

CHAPTER 10

Living and Loving as Your True Self

"The Western woman will save the world."
—The Dalai Lama (2009 Vancouver Peace Summit)

I saw this quotation hanging on a wall in a wellness center I was working with in 2011. It hit me hard. I thought, *That's me!* His words pointed to the power and privilege I possess and hadn't recognized. I felt an obligation to do something with those gifts. I also felt excitement and motivation to step up my game. I'd somehow been given permission to claim my talents and abilities and use them in the world!

You, too, are allowed to be the most expanded version of yourself. In fact, you are the only one who can share all the talents and abilities that are unique to you. Your full true self is needed now. Your gifts of sensitivity, empathy, and intuition are exactly what the world needs more of. These abilities are your super-powers! Once you start to trust them, you can rely on them to give you a fuller picture of what is right for you in each moment.

> "Our deepest fear is not that we are inade-quate. Our deepest fear is that we are powerful beyond measure. It is our light, not our dark-ness, that most frightens us. We ask ourselves, 'Who am I to be brilliant, gorgeous, talented, fabulous?' Actually, who are you not to be?"
>
> —Marianne Williamson, *A Return to Love: Reflections on the Principles of "A Course in Miracles"*

Move toward and attend to your excitement and joy. What lights you up? What, who and where feels good to you? What feels like home, feels exciting or feels natural to you? You're allowed to follow your feelings. Your heart will always lead you toward a truer version of yourself. It is your right to be happy, free and loved and to pursue a life that reflects who you are. As you grow into your true self, your view of what is possible will expand so you can create a life you love.

Self-Love

Mirror Work

To see, know and appreciate your true self, develop a deep connection with yourself, and live with self-respect and self-love

1. **Take** a few minutes each morning to stop what you're doing in front of the bathroom mirror and look into your eyes.

2. **If** your gaze strays to other parts of your face, just bring it back to your own eyes.

3. **Allow** emotions to arise.

4. **Remain** steady and dive deeper into your own gaze.

5. **Ask** yourself: Who is in there? What is she feeling? What does she need right now?

6. **If** it's difficult to hold your gaze for more than a few seconds, look away for a moment and then try again.

7. **Notice** what it feels like to watch your own emotions.

8. **Practice** "mirror work" daily even for just a few minutes.

As you do this, you may see various types of pain cross your face like sadness, loneliness, fear, or disappointment. This may be the first time you are acknowledging such deep emotions, many of which have built up through your entire life. For me, I was seeing a lonely, scared little girl who was just trying to get by in life. Looking into my own eyes, there was no way to deny my pain anymore. It had been just below the surface all along.

Self-Trust Journaling

To identify and trust your inherent sensitive, intuitive, and/or empathic abilities, honor all parts of yourself, and live-in integrity

1. **In** the evening, sit in a quiet place with your journal, get comfortable, and breathe.

2. **Review** your day and write down the answers to the following questions:

   • **When** and where did you notice one of your unique abilities? Describe the situation.

   • **How** did you behave and/or express yourself in that moment?

   • **Is** there anything you wish you had done or said but didn't? For example, did you deny your intuitive feeling to avoid making someone uncomfortable? Did you shrink in response to feeling sensitive instead of bravely speaking up? Did you hide your empathy because you thought you might be perceived as overly emotional?

   • **At** the times you were able to express yourself, how did that feel?

Do this journaling daily for a few weeks to draw your attention to where you want to change your patterns.

Values Visualization

To identify the values that reflect your true self and to gain clarity about what is truly meaningful for you

1. **Get** comfortable in a chair or lie down; have your journal close by.

2. **Close** your eyes, drop into your body, and notice your breathing. Take a few breaths to quiet your mind.

3. **Relax** into the creative, playful, imaginative part of your mind.

4. **Imagine** that a new planet has been discovered and you are in charge of deciding what kind of civilization to build there.

5. **Visualize** all the aspects of this new civilization.

6. **Imagine** the highest dreams for yourself, your loved ones, and the world.

7. **What** would this new world look and feel like?

8. **How** would people live, work, play, and love?

9. **How** would people behave and treat each other?

10. **Open** your eyes and write down common themes from your answers to the above questions. For example, you might notice that community is important to you.

11. **Find** the relationship between these themes and your values. For example, if community is a theme, you may value kindness, fairness, cooperation, and/ or service.

12. **Go** back through your answers and identify your top three values.

13. **Write** them down and sit with them for a few minutes. Breathe, relax your body, and feel your resonance with these words. You are discovering a significant part of your unique self to honor and love.

Self-Compassion

As you experiment with being more self-loving, it will be necessary to also cultivate self-compassion. Your comfort and care will become your top priority as you treat yourself with kindness and gentleness. And as you find yourself worthy of your own compassion, your self-worth will soar. You will understand—maybe for the first time—that you are truly free to live your life your way. This takes a daily practice of believing and trusting your body's wisdom and then acting on what your body needs.

Allow your body sensations—especially your heart—to speak louder than your mind. Practice compassionate self-awareness each moment. Notice how your body reacts to various people, information, and situations. Then with kindness and respect for yourself, act on what you notice as much as you are able. Remember: baby steps! For example, one thing I noticed about myself is that my upper lip curls up when I don't like something. When I first started noticing this, I questioned whether this physical reaction was a reliable indicator of my preferences. But once I paid attention and then trusted the message my body was sending me, I realized that the lip curl meant, "Don't go in that direction. It's not for you." I was then able to make quicker and wiser decisions about what to do when I got this message. This minor reaction could easily have gone unnoticed, but when I became aware of it, I received some important information.

This kind of self-awareness practice will reveal habitual thoughts and beliefs that cause self-doubt, guilt, and/or anxiety. Each time you practice listening and responding to your body sensations, you will have the opportunity to practice self-compassion around the emotions they bring up. Developing self-compassion happens in each moment you choose to be aware of how you are feeling and thinking. You'll be amazed, for example, at how often you are mean to yourself! You may have been raised with negative reinforcement like anger, name-calling, judgment, and criticism. As you grew up, you continued to speak to yourself in the same way and believe those messages. When you start to sense (through your body) the immediate reality of a situation—including your energy level, ability, and desire—it becomes easier to take the pressure off and give yourself some grace. This is moment-to-moment self-compassion. The following healing processes will help you consider your own needs and wants, trust your own wisdom, and learn to be self-compassionate and kind.

Self-Talk Journaling

To shift from judging, criticizing, or doubting yourself to reassuring yourself

1. **Sit** down with your journal at the end of the day, breathe, and relax your body.

2. **Call** to mind an episode when you were unkind to yourself. Perhaps you judged your work as inadequate, or you doubted your own emotions, thoughts, or ideas.

3. **What** was your tone of voice? Did you speak out loud or in your mind?

4. **If** you were critical of yourself, how would you speak to a friend in the same situation?

5. **Carefully** considering your energy level, thinking ability, and mood, what were you truly capable of today? Be honest. Watch out for, "I should have been able to…"

6. **What** were you feeling during this episode? Frustrated, tired, overwhelmed?

7. **Write** down some reassuring statements to say to yourself such as, "I'm allowed to feel my emotions." "I have permission to rest when I need to." "I'm happy going at my own pace." "My emotions, thoughts, and ideas are valid and worth exploring."

Daily Mindfulness Practice

To raise your awareness, slow down, and get off autopilot so you can be present with your thoughts, feelings and emotions

- **Notice** where your attention goes during your daily activities.

- **Refocus** your attention on how you feel and what you are doing in the moment, not on what needs to be done.

- **Notice** your body sensations, facial expressions, mood, and attitude.

- **Notice** your inner dialogue.

- **Mindfully** take note of your reactions and how each activity or situation affects you.

- **Journal** what you notice. Maybe you are more exhausted or anxious than you realize, and you've been ignoring that information to keep going.

Make a commitment to practice daily by setting an intention each morning, for example, "I will pay attention to how I am feeling today." Take breathing breaks throughout the day to refocus on the present moment.

A Practice for Trying New Things

To become aware of what interests and activities feel good to you and to bring them more fully into your life

- **Allow** yourself to stop doing something that doesn't feel good.

- **Avoid** judging or pushing yourself.

- **Ask** yourself, "Out of all the things I need to do today, what do I really want to do? What else do I want to do that I haven't scheduled in? What do I want to delegate to someone else or just drop altogether?"

- **Now** ask yourself, "What new things do I want to try?"

- **Mindfully** notice how it feels to take baby steps in a new direction, with the attitude of experimentation and a sense of curiosity.

With this practice, identifying a new direction and taking small steps forward is your only goal – not finishing something, doing it well, or having someone else approve of it. This is about slowly building a life that reflects your true self.

Meditation to Connect with Your Higher Self

To connect with and receive your own personal wisdom

Sit or lay down in a quiet space. Close your eyes. Have your journal nearby.

- **Begin** to breathe slowly and deeply for a few minutes to settle your body.

- **Say** out loud, "Higher self, I need help."

- **Start** to whisper, or ponder quietly in your mind, these questions:

  - **What** are my talents and abilities?
  - **What** are my longings and dreams?
  - **What** is in my highest good?
  - **What** is my highest potential?

- **With** each question, wait quietly for answers to come to you. Your mind may want to chime in with thoughts and ideas. Let them pass by for now.

- **Wait** and listen.

- **Answers** may come that cause emotions to surface. This is a sign you are on the right track. Do not analyze or doubt them. Just feel them.

- **Continue** for a few minutes or as long as you are comfortable.

- **When** you feel that you are finished, open your eyes and journal what you learned and felt.

Create a Life You Love

Freedom

I've come to believe that fear is man-made. The acronym I use for fear is *False Evidence Appearing Real*. There is nothing in the world we need to fear. It's the messages we absorb about the world from our family and society at large that cause fear. Our natural state is freedom where we trust ourselves, each other, and our environment. You can carefully and compassionately let go of messages and beliefs that disturb you. You can choose to live from your heart, trusting that your life is unfolding as it is meant to.

Claim your sovereignty as a soul. You are free to pursue a life that represents your unique soul expression. This is your birthright. If you want to live in a way that is different from your family and friends, then try it. Most likely, you have all the skills you need, or you wouldn't be dreaming about it. That's how our soul and body work together: You chose this family, this body, this location, and this time for your soul's expression. Be the trailblazer you are meant to be. Dreams are meant to be followed. Any thoughts or beliefs that are stopping you point directly to areas where you need to heal. It's a beautifully perfect system of awareness and opportunity when you learn to trust it, and it only works in baby steps. When you come up against a block, heal it. Then you will see the next step.

Creativity

Creating is part of your healing path. What unique contribution will you create for yourself and the world using your newly discovered talents, abilities, strengths, and capabilities? We learn more about ourselves in the creative process. We learn to try new things, being gentle with ourselves in uncertainty and trying again without judgment. When a creative effort brings up lessons and challenges, address them as part of your emotional healing. Trust that this can be an effortless process when you flow with it, using your resources and those around you. Build. Contribute. Amplify new ideas and serve the world. Create with love and joy as a way of celebrating your life, enjoying yourself, and expanding your life experience. This is how you light the way for others—daring to be your true self and holding the space for others to do the same.

A New World

As we each create a life we love, we are together creating a new world. We need more heart-centered women (and men) who trust their innate gifts of intuition, sensitivity and empathy to spread love, care and compassion in the world. Then others will feel supported and encouraged to explore and express their unique talents and authentic selves as well. We are missing the confident expression of the feminine in the world. As women heal their emotions and live with an open heart, more grounded feminine energy will be released into the world. We will clearly and reverently know, honor and use our abilities of caring, flexibility, patience, communication and sharing.

> You are the agent of peace, nurturing, abundance, beauty, and inspiration. You either express these values or you don't. The choice involves a conscious decision, and when enough people make the decision, the world will change. Everyone needs to look to the divine feminine. This is the dominant challenge that faces every society, and the future of humanity depends upon meeting the challenge as consciously and as soon as possible.
>
> —Deepak Chopra, Special to SFGate.

The masculine and feminine energies are out of balance. We must raise the feminine aspects like cooperation, intuition, and community to counterbalance the dominant masculine aspects of competition, logic, and individualism. Women (and men) embracing and celebrating these feminine aspects are the change agents who will usher in a new, harmonious world. Anything is possible as more and more people start on this path. Are you ready to create this new world with me? Can I count on you to step up in your unique way? Ignore any lingering doubt. It's time to create the life you've dreamed of. You are needed to help this shift happen. The new world I dream of includes all of you.

Resources

Books

Psychology

Adult Children of Emotionally Immature Parents
Lindsay Gibson, PhD

Running on Empty
Dr. Jonice Webb

Surviving a Borderline Parent
Kimberly Roth and Freda Friedman, PhD, LCSW

Gifts of Imperfection
Dr. Brené Brown

Daring Greatly
Dr. Brené Brown

Braving the Wilderness
Dr. Brené Brown

Journey into Healing
Deepak Chopra, MD

Hold On to Your Kids
Gabor Maté, MD

Healing Collective Trauma
Thomas Hübl

The 5 Love Languages
Gary Chapman

The Four Agreements
Don Miguel Ruiz

Spirituality

A New Earth
Eckhart Tolle

Women Who Run With the Wolves
Clarissa Pinkola Estes, PhD

Creative Visualization
Shakti Gawain

Siddhartha
Hermann Hesse

Bhagavad Gita
translation by Stephen Mitchell

Anatomy of a Spirit
Caroline Myss, PhD

Why People Don't Heal and How They Can
Caroline Myss, PhD

The Seven Spiritual Laws of Success
Deepak Chopra, MD

The Dance
Oriah

The Untethered Soul
Michael A. Singer

Journey to the Heart
Melody Beattie

Biology

Biology of Belief
Bruce Lipton, PhD

Molecules of Emotion
Candace Pert, PhD

Women's Bodies, Women's Wisdom
Christiane Northrup, MD

Organizations

American Holistic Nurses Association
https://www.ahna.org

Integrative Practitioner
https://www.integrativepractitioner.com

The HeartMath Institute
https://www.heartmath.org

Co-Active Training Institute
https://coactive.com

Lee Harris Energy
https://www.leeharrisenergy.com

Recommended Tools and Practices

Yoga

- Ashtanga Yoga – A specific system using a series of poses; more vigorous; good for deep breath work, strength building, and stress reduction.

- Vinyasa Yoga – A practice of flowing through poses; good for coordination, breath work, and balancing the mind and body.

- Yin Yoga – A slower-paced practice; longer holds in supported poses; good for stretching, cooling, and calming the nervous system.

Energy Healing

- Usui Reiki – Healing energy is transferred through a practitioner's hands into the client's body to ease tension and stress and facilitate healing at the physical, emotional, and spiritual levels.

- Acupuncture – Traditional Chinese Medicine (TCM) techniques are used to stimulate the meridians of the body with thin needles to balance energy flow; may reduce anxiety, improve energy, and reduce pain.

- Craniosacral Therapy – Gentle, hands-on technique that relieves restrictions in tissues around the central nervous system that affect the craniosacral system. Enhances the body's ability to self-correct; helps with stress, tension, and fatigue.

- Aromatherapy – Inhalation of essential oils to promote relaxation, sleep, and relief from fatigue. Can easily be used with meditation and massage through candles and diffusers. Lavender, lemon balm, calendula, and sandalwood all have a calming effect.

- Swedish Massage – Therapeutic, full-body, soft tissue massage relieves muscle tension that commonly accompanies anxiety. Facilitates ease of movement and promotes relaxation.

Meditation

A daily meditation practice trains the body to breathe deeply and fully, quiets the mind, relieves muscle tension, facilitates the mind/body connection, and promotes present-moment awareness. Trying a variety of guided meditations is a good way to build a meditation practice before you try silent meditation.

The Insight Timer app (www.insighttimer.com) has over sixty thousand high-quality meditations to choose from so you can explore and discover what type of meditation works best for you. New free tracks are frequently added. It has an extensive free version as well as a Member Plus subscription for $59.99 per year or $9.99 a month. Following is a sample of some of the featured meditations:

- Mindfulness meditation

- Breathing meditation

- Sleep meditation

- Anxiety-relief meditation

- Self-love meditation

- Healing meditation

- Morning meditation

- Yoga Nidra meditation

- Loving-kindness meditation

- Heart Connection meditation

- Moon meditation

~

About the Author

Andrea Paquette, MSN, APRN, is board certified as a Pediatric Nurse Practitioner and a Holistic Nurse Practitioner. She specializes in natural treatments for emotional and mental health issues in women, adolescents, and children. Her private practice is located in Londonderry, NH.

While treating children in her private practice, she recognized the need among mothers for new strategies to cope with chronic stress, low energy, and feeling disempowered. In 2018, Andrea completed training as a Life Coach and began coaching and teaching women to express their authentic selves, use their talents in the world, and create a life they love. Her coaching business is Woman to Woman Life Coaching.

Andrea also has extensive experience teaching and speaking about personal development, spiritual growth, parenting, and child emotional health. She has developed and taught several programs, workshops, and classes on varied topics over several years. She continues to speak to community groups, professional organizations, and schools around New Hampshire.

With over thirty years of experience in the healthcare field, Andrea's mission is to support people on their journey to vibrant physical and emotional health, happiness, and fulfillment in life. Andrea lives in Manchester, NH, has two grown children she adores, is a devoted yoga student and an ocean and food lover.

Website: https://andreapaquettenp.com
Writing: https://www.elephantjournal.com/profile/andrea-paquette/

Social media

- **Facebook:** https://www.facebook.com/andreapaquettellc

- **Instagram:** https://www.instagram.com/anpaq03/

- **LinkedIn:** https://www.linkedin.com/in/andrea-paquette-aprn-pnp-bc-aphn-bc-08b50822/

Directories

- **Women's** Wellness Exchange: https://www.womenswellnessxchange.com/united-states/services-products/woman-to-woman-coaching-andrea-paquette-llc

- **American** Holistic Nurses Credentialing Center: https://www.ahncc.org/cia-overview/cia-business/

viii | PREFACE

University of Singapore before his death in 2013, were both generous in exchanges about the rural Northeast based not only on my research but also on their own studies of rural northeastern Thailand.

Suriya Smutkupt, who taught at both Khon Kaen University and Suranaree University of Technology in Khorat, has been our long-term research partner and has assisted us on many occasions. He has significantly influenced my thinking through our exchanges based on his very impressive knowledge of rural Isan.

In recent years I have also had many fruitful exchanges with our son, Nick (Nicholas) Keyes, and his wife, Mem (Uayporn Satitpanyapan), who have much more urban perspectives on Thai society but who also respect Jane's and my deep attachment to the rural Northeast. Jonathan, our younger son, spent time with us in "our" village in Maha Sarakham in 1983, and his wife, Kate, later visited Ban Nong Tuen. I am very indebted to our family for the interest and support they have shown in Jane's and my abiding relationship with rural Isan.

My research would not have been possible without the financial support I have received over the years from Cornell University, the Ford Foundation, the Social Science Research Foundation, the University of Washington, as well as sponsorship by the National Research Council of Thailand and by Khon Kaen, Maha Sarakham, and Chiang Mai Universities.

In the end, I recognize that I am ultimately responsible for what appears here. I can only hope that the book makes some contribution not only to a better understanding of how rural northeastern Thailand—rural Isan—has contributed to the shaping of the transformed and transforming nation-state of Thailand, but also to an understanding of the "rural" as is manifest more widely in the early twenty-first century.

Portland, Oregon
November 2013